CLB 1638
© 1986 Illustrations and text: Colour Library Books Ltd.,
   Guildford, Surrey, England.
Printed and bound in Barcelona, Spain.
All rights reserved.
ISBN 0 86283 229 3 (Hardback)
ISBN 0 86283 295 0 (Softback)

Text by
Lalita Ahmed
Photography by
Peter Barry
Designed by
Philip Clucas
Produced by
Ted Smart and Gerald Hughes
Editorial Direction
David Gibbon

VEGETARIAN
COOKING

COLOUR LIBRARY BOOKS

Mixed Vegetables in Yogurt (top), Noodles (below left) and New Potato Fry (bottom right).

Contents

This page: Greenbeans with Coconut (top) and Spinach with Paneer (above). Facing page: Vegetable Stir Fry.

Introduction

It is amazing how rigid we are when it comes to the subject of food and what we eat. In all other aspects of life virtually anything goes: people walk the streets with pink hair; sail the Atlantic single-handed or jog around the houses for two hours every morning and yet if we prefer beans and lentils to beef and chicken we are considered as being rather odd.

Vegetarians are not cranks, and there is nothing weird and wonderful about a pattern of vegetarian eating; they just prefer to eat dishes which do not contain meat, poultry, game and, quite often, fish. 'Why don't they become ill?' you hear people say; 'Where do they get their energy from if they don't eat meat?'; 'How boring to live on just vegetables and those little dried peas!' As vegetarians will happily tell you, they feel perfectly healthy, have quite sufficient energy to cope with day-to-day activities and, above all, *they really enjoy their food.*

A vegetarian diet can be just as varied and interesting as one based on meat and fish. Meat is much the same the world over, which cannot be said of the wide and wonderful range of fresh fruits and vegetables. And it is variety which is very much the keynote of vegetarian eating: different pastas, rices, cheeses, nuts and pulses are just a selection of the varied ingredients of a vegetarian diet. Most important of all, vegetarian dishes are every bit as nutritious as their meat-rich counterparts. The main difference lies with the types of food which provide us with the necessary nutrients. In a typical vegetarian dish, the protein usually comes from pulses, nuts or cheese, or a combination of these ingredients. Minerals, vitamins, fats and carbohydrates come from all the other basic foods, such as those already mentioned.

Eating 'the vegetarian way' has all sorts of advantages in its favour. A meatless diet is a very healthy one since it is nutritious, low in fat and high in bulk and fibre. Vegetarians rarely need to watch their weight as a diet that is high in natural fibre and low in fat is comparatively low in calories. The traditional pattern of Western eating is relatively expensive to follow, whereas vegetarian dishes are more economical to prepare and cook. In fact, meatless meals can simply make a nice change from the traditional pattern of eating. Vegetarian cooking is fun, and eating vegetarian meals is healthy and good for you.

Vegetarian food really can be exciting and delicious and even if you are not a committed vegetarian many of the ideas in this book are well worth trying. The dishes combine unusual tastes and textures with an imaginative use of spices and fresh herbs for extra flavour. If you served many of the recipes to your family and friends they probably wouldn't even realise that their meal was meatless.

Soups

Cucumber Soup

PREPARATION TIME: 15 minutes

COOKING TIME: 8-10 minutes

SERVES: 4 people

1 large cucumber
250ml (8 fl oz) water
600ml (1 pint) vegetable stock
15ml (1 tblsp) white wine vinegar
30ml (2 tblsp) cornflour mixed with
30ml (2 tblsp) water
30ml (2 tblsp) soured cream
30ml (2 tblsp) natural yogurt
Salt and ground white pepper to taste
15ml (1 tblsp) chopped chives or
    green spring onion tops
Chilli powder

Cut ¼ of the cucumber into wafer thin rounds and keep aside for garnishing. Puree the rest of the cucumber with the water in a liquidiser. Put the chicken stock and the pureed cucumber into a saucepan and bring to the boil over a medium heat. Add the vinegar and cook for 1 minute. Add the cornflour mixture gradually. Stir well until the soup starts to thicken. Simmer for 2-3 minutes. Remove from the heat and cool slightly. Blend in the liquidiser and add the soured cream and yogurt. Return to the saucepan and season with salt and pepper. Heat through gently to serve hot or chill to serve cold. Serve garnished with sliced cucumber and chopped chives or spring onion tops. Sprinkle with chilli powder.

Daal Soup

This is a thick and hearty soup, made from lentils. The lentils most often used for making soup are red lentils, or yellow lentils which are called Toor daal. The recipe below can be made with either variety.

PREPARATION TIME: 15-20
    minutes

COOKING TIME: 15 minutes

SERVES: 4-6 people

350g (12oz) red lentils (see above)
900ml (1½ pints) water
4 canned tomatoes, drained and
    crushed

1 green chilli, sliced lengthways and
    seeded
30ml (2 tblsp) natural yogurt or
    soured cream
15g (½oz) butter
1 medium onion, peeled and chopped
salt and freshly ground black pepper
    to taste
1-2 sprigs fresh green coriander
    leaves, chopped

Wash the lentils in 4-5 changes of water. Drain the lentils and put them into a pan with the water. Cover the pan and bring to the boil; simmer for 10 minutes. Beat until smooth with an egg whisk. Add the crushed tomatoes and green chilli and simmer gently for 2 minutes. Stir in the yogurt or soured cream. Melt the butter in a small pan and fry the onion until golden. Season the hot soup with salt and pepper and pour into a serving bowl; sprinkle with the fried onion and chopped coriander. Serve immediately with buttered brown bread, crisp rolls or croutons.

Tomato Saar

This is a thin tomato soup from the South of India. It makes a refreshing and interesting starter.

PREPARATION TIME: 15 minutes

COOKING TIME: 17-18 minutes

SERVES: 4-6 people

10ml (2 tsp) butter
1 small onion, peeled and chopped
225g (½lb) tomatoes, skinned and
    chopped
1 litre (1¾ pints) water
15ml (1 tblsp) tomato puree
4-6 green curry leaves
Salt and freshly ground black pepper
    to taste
3 cloves of garlic, peeled and crushed

Garnish

1-2 sprigs fresh green coriander or
    parsley leaves, chopped
1 green chilli, chopped (optional)

Melt half of the butter and fry the onion for 3-4 minutes. Add the skinned and chopped tomatoes and cook for 5 minutes. Blend the water and tomato puree and add to the onion and tomatoes. Add curry leaves. Season with salt and pepper. Cover and simmer for 5-7 minutes. Heat the remaining butter and fry the crushed cloves of garlic until dark brown. Pour the mixture over the simmering tomato soup. Remove from the heat. Sprinkle over the chopped coriander and chilli. Discard green chilli before eating. Serve piping hot either with French bread or with a little plain boiled rice. Alternatively: blend the skinned tomatoes to give a smooth textured soup.

Mixed Vegetable Soup

This Indian recipe can include a wide variety of vegetables. One creates one's own dish by adding or subtracting one or more vegetables.

PREPARATION TIME: 15 minutes

COOKING TIME: about 20 minutes

SERVES: 6 people

10ml (2 tsp) butter
1 medium onion, peeled and chopped
6 cloves
2.5cm (1 inch) piece cinnamon stick
4 small green cardamoms
1 small bayleaf
1 medium potato, peeled and
    chopped
2 carrots, peeled and chopped
1 banana, peeled and chopped
6 florets of cauliflower
50g (2oz) shelled fresh or frozen peas
1 leek, washed and chopped
1 stick celery, chopped
50g (2oz) green beans (sliced or
    chopped)
1 litre (1¾ pints) water
Salt and freshly ground black pepper
    to taste

Garnish

1-2 sprigs fresh green coriander
1-2 green chillies chopped

Melt the butter in a large saucepan and fry the onion for 3 minutes. Add the cloves, cinnamon, cardamom, bayleaf and fry for 1 minute. Add the potato, carrots, banana and cauliflower. Fry for 3 minutes. Add the remaining vegetables and cook for 2-3 minutes. Add water and salt and pepper to taste. Cover and simmer gently for 8-13 minutes until vegetables are cooked. Adjust seasoning. Garnish with chopped coriander leaves and green chillies. Discard green chillies before eating. The vegetables should float in the clear soup; do not blend.

Carrot Soup

PREPARATION TIME: 12 minutes

COOKING TIME: 20-25 minutes

SERVES: 4 people

4-6 carrots, peeled and cut into thick
    slices
1 medium onion, peeled and
    quartered
1 medium turnip, peeled and cut into
    wedges
2 cloves garlic, peeled
750ml (1¼ pints) water or chicken
    stock
2.5ml (½ tsp) dried thyme
Salt and ground white pepper to taste
Hot pepper sauce to taste

Garnish

25g (1oz) toasted sunflower seeds,
    flaked almonds and pistachio nuts
    (mixed together)

Put the carrots, onion, turnip, garlic and water into a large saucepan. Cover and simmer for 15 minutes. Add thyme and salt and pepper to taste and simmer for a further 5 minutes. Cool slightly and blend in a liquidiser. Return to the saucepan and heat the soup through. Ladle the soup into bowls. Add hot pepper sauce to taste. Serve garnished with toasted nuts.

**Facing page: Tomato Saar (top
right), Daal Soup (centre left)
and Mixed Vegetable Soup
(bottom).**

Minestrone Soup

This famous vegetable and pasta soup from Italy can be made in many different ways. The recipe below is a simple, but delicious one – served with bread, it is a complete meal in itself.

PREPARATION TIME: 20 minutes
COOKING TIME: 30 minutes
SERVES: 4-6 people

45ml (3 tblsp) olive oil
1 medium onion, peeled and chopped
2 cloves of garlic, peeled and crushed
2 medium potatoes, peeled and diced
3 carrots, peeled and diced
2 stems celery, chopped
175g (6oz) shredded cabbage
4-5 skinned or canned tomatoes, chopped
900ml (1½ pints) water or vegetable stock
1 bouquet garni

Quick Tomato Soup (above right), Minestrone Soup (right) and Onion Soup (far right).

175g (6oz) shelled fresh, or frozen
  peas
50g (2oz) boiled and cooked red
  kidney beans
100g (4oz) macaroni or any shaped
  pasta
Salt and freshly ground black pepper
  to taste
50g (2oz) grated Parmesan cheese

Heat the olive oil in a saucepan and fry the onion and garlic until the onion is soft, 2-3 minutes. Stir in the potatoes, carrots and celery and fry for 3 minutes; add the cabbage and tomatoes. Cook for 5-6 minutes. Add water or stock and bouquet garni. Add peas, kidney beans, pasta and simmer gently, covered, for 10-15 minutes, or until the pasta is just tender. Season with salt and pepper and ladle into bowls. Sprinkle generously with grated Parmesan cheese before serving. Serve Minestrone soup with crusty bread.

Quick Tomato Soup

This is quite an exotic soup and is made within a few minutes. It is ideal for a hot summer's day.

PREPARATION TIME: 10 minutes
plus chilling time

SERVES: 4-6 people

600ml (1 pint) chilled tomato juice
50g (2oz) fresh or canned tomato
  puree, chilled
2.5ml (½ tsp) hot red pepper sauce
2.5ml (½ tsp) grated lemon peel
2.5ml (½ tsp) grated orange peel
45-60ml (3-4 tblsp) dry white wine
Salt and ground white pepper to taste
Little iced water
45ml (3 tblsp) natural yogurt
60ml (4 tblsp) soured cream
6 balls of honeydew melon
6 balls of water melon
6 balls of ripe pear

Garnish
Mint leaves

Mix the tomato juice, tomato puree, pepper sauce, fruit peels and wine together. Season with salt and pepper, cover and refrigerate for 3-4 hours. Thin the soup with a little iced water if necessary. Whisk the yogurt and cream together until smooth and light. Divide the soup amongst 4-6 bowls. Spoon the yogurt and cream mixture into the centre of each portion and float the fruit balls on top. Garnish with mint leaves and serve.

Rice and Mushroom Soup

Ideal for a party or for summer afternoons.

PREPARATION TIME: 10 minutes

COOKING TIME: 40-50 minutes

SERVES: 6-8 people

125g (4oz) wild rice or brown rice
250ml (8 fl oz) water
25g (1oz) butter
1 medium onion, peeled and finely
  chopped
1 stem celery, chopped
100g (4oz) mushrooms, chopped
2.5ml (½ tsp) powdered garam
  masala
2.5ml (½ tsp) ground mustard seed
Salt and freshly ground black pepper
  to taste
1 litre (1¾ pints) water or stock
22ml (1½ tblsp) cornflour blended
  with
30ml (2 tblsp) water
75ml (5 tblsp) single cream

Garnish
1-2 sprigs fresh green coriander or
  parsley, chopped

Wash the rice in 3-4 changes of water; cook covered in 250ml (8 fl oz) water for 25-30 minutes, or until rice is tender. Keep on one side. Melt the butter in a large saucepan; saute the onion until tender for 3-5 minutes. Add the celery and mushrooms. Cook for 1-2 minutes. Stir in the powdered garam masala, mustard and salt and pepper to taste. Add the water or stock. Simmer for 5 minutes. Add the cornflour mixture and simmer for a further 3 minutes. Add the cooked rice and cream. Gently stir over a low heat for 2 minutes to heat through. Ladle the soup into bowls and garnish with coriander or parsley.

Onion Soup

Onion soup has been made famous by the French. Here is a delicious recipe based on the French style.

PREPARATION TIME: 20 minutes

COOKING TIME: 1 hour

SERVES: 4-6 people

75g (3oz) butter
3-4 large onions, peeled and sliced
  into rings
30ml (2 tblsp) flour
900ml (1½ pints) vegetable stock

Salt and ground white pepper to taste
6 slices of French bread 1½cm
  (¾ inch) thick
2 cloves of garlic, peeled and bruised
75g (3oz) grated Parmesan cheese

Melt the butter in a saucepan and fry the onions briskly on a very low heat. Cover and simmer the onions in their own juices for 25-30 minutes, stirring occasionally until golden brown. Remove from the heat. Stir in the flour and add the stock gradually. Season with salt

and pepper and return to heat. Bring to the boil quickly; reduce the heat and simmer covered for 15-20 minutes. Rub the bread pieces each side with the bruised garlic. Float the bread rounds in the soup and sprinkle grated Parmesan cheese generously over the top. Put under the grill and cook for 2-3 minutes or until the top is golden. Serve at once. Alternatively – fry the bread rounds or bread slices in butter prior to rubbing with garlic.

Carrot Soup (top), Rice and Mushroom Soup (centre right) and Cucumber Soup (bottom left).

Snacks and Starters

Flour Pancake

This is a favourite pancake from the southern part of India and it is really worth making; good, wholesome and nutritious.

PREPARATION TIME: 10 minutes

COOKING TIME: 20 minutes

SERVES: 6 people

275g (10oz) wholemeal flour
2.5ml (½ tsp) salt
150ml (¼ pint) natural yogurt
1 egg, beaten
1 small onion, peeled and chopped
1-2 green chillies, chopped
2 sprigs fresh green coriander leaves, chopped
15ml (1 tblsp) grated fresh coconut, or desiccated coconut
10ml (2 tsp) sugar
Olive oil

Sieve the flour and salt and add the yogurt and egg. Mix in sufficient water to make a thickish batter of pouring consistency. Beat the mixture well and add the onion, chilli, coriander, coconut and sugar. Mix well. Allow to stand for 2-3 minutes. Heat 15ml (1 tblsp) oil in a small frying pan or omelette pan. Spoon in a little of the batter to give a depth of 5mm (1¼ inch). Cover with a lid and cook over a low heat for 3-5 minutes. Turn the pancake over and pour a little oil around the edge; cover and cook until the pancake is set and brown on both sides. Repeat with the remaining batter until you have several pancakes. Serve piping hot.

Dosas

Dosas can be eaten plain or with a filling. Eat them as a snack, for breakfast, or as a main meal with a filling and accompanied by chutney and daal (lentil dish).

PREPARATION TIME: overnight, plus 20 minutes

COOKING TIME: 30-45 minutes

SERVES: 6 people

450g (1lb) rice
225g (½lb) white lentils (urid daal)
1.25ml (¼ tsp) fenugreek seeds

5ml (1 tsp) dried yeast
5ml (1 tsp) sugar
2.5ml (½ tsp) salt
15ml (1 tblsp) natural yogurt
Olive oil

Wash the rice and white lentils separately in 3-4 changes of water. Soak in fresh water for 1 hour. Grind the rice with a little water to a thick, coarse paste. Grind the white lentils with fenugreek seeds and a little water into a fine paste. (Use a food processor, food liquidiser or food grinder). Mix the dried yeast with 15ml (1 tblsp) tepid water and the sugar. Mix well and leave to stand for 10 minutes until frothy. Mix the ground rice and lentils with the salt, yeast and yogurt and mix well. Cover with a cloth and leave in a dark, warm place overnight. Next day mix well with sufficient water to give a smooth, thickish batter. Heat a medium non-stick frying pan and grease well with 5ml (1 tsp) oil. Pour in 30-45ml (2-3 tblsp) of the

Baisen Omelette (top right), Flour Pancake (centre left) and Dosas (bottom).

rice batter, spread it around to make a thin pancake. Cover with a lid. Cook for 3-4 minutes; spoon a little oil around the edge of the frying pan and turn the dosa over.

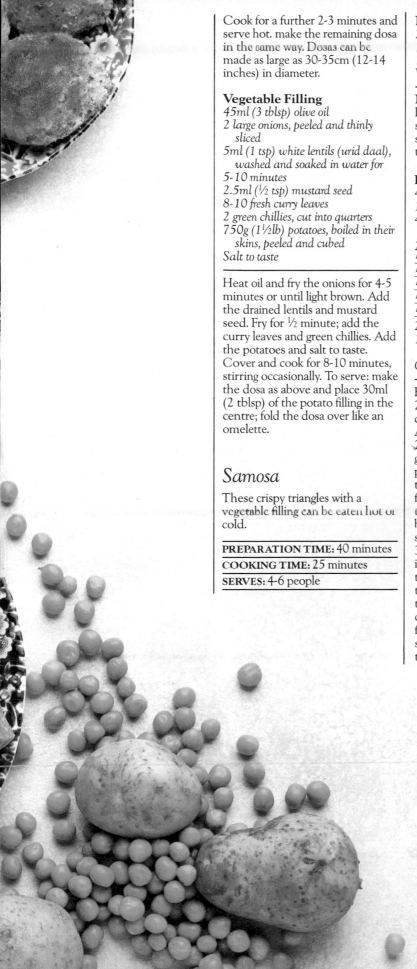

Cook for a further 2-3 minutes and serve hot. make the remaining dosa in the same way. Dosas can be made as large as 30-35cm (12-14 inches) in diameter.

Vegetable Filling

45ml (3 tblsp) olive oil
2 large onions, peeled and thinly sliced
5ml (1 tsp) white lentils (urid daal), washed and soaked in water for 5-10 minutes
2.5ml (½ tsp) mustard seed
8-10 fresh curry leaves
2 green chillies, cut into quarters
750g (1½lb) potatoes, boiled in their skins, peeled and cubed
Salt to taste

Heat oil and fry the onions for 4-5 minutes or until light brown. Add the drained lentils and mustard seed. Fry for ½ minute; add the curry leaves and green chillies. Add the potatoes and salt to taste. Cover and cook for 8-10 minutes, stirring occasionally. To serve: make the dosa as above and place 30ml (2 tblsp) of the potato filling in the centre; fold the dosa over like an omelette.

Samosa

These crispy triangles with a vegetable filling can be eaten hot or cold.

PREPARATION TIME: 40 minutes
COOKING TIME: 25 minutes
SERVES: 4-6 people

Pastry

275g (10oz) plain flour, sieved
1.25ml (¼ tsp) salt
1.25ml (¼ tsp) baking powder
Water

Make the dough by adding water, a little at a time, to the sieved flour, salt and baking powder. Mix to a soft pliable dough. Cover and allow to stand.

Filling

45ml (3 tblsp) oil
1 medium onion, peeled and chopped
450g (1lb) potatoes, peeled and cubed
2 carrots, peeled and grated
50g (2oz) shelled green peas
50g (2oz) green beans, chopped
5ml (1 tsp) chilli powder
5ml (1 tsp) salt
5ml (1 tsp) garam masala powder
2.5ml (½ tsp) ground turmeric
15ml (1 tblsp) dry mango powder, or lemon juice
Oil for deep frying

Heat the oil and fry the onions for 2-3 minutes. Add the potatoes and carrots and cook for 3 minutes. Add peas and beans and cook for 2-3 minutes. Sprinkle chilli, salt, garam masala, turmeric and mango powder. Mix well, cover and cook till potatoes are tender. Remove from heat and allow to cool. Divide the dough into 12-14 equal sized balls; roll each one out on a floured surface to a thin circle, 6-7cm (2½-3 inch) in diameter. Cut each circle in half. Apply the flour paste on the straight edge of each half. bring the edges together, overlapping them so as to make a cone. Fill the cone with the filling. Apply a little flour paste on the open edge and seal by pressing both the edges together. This will make a

triangular shape. Make all the samosas in the same way. Heat the oil for deep frying. When the oil is hot, reduce the heat and fry the samosas, a few at a time, until golden brown on either side (about 4-5 minutes). Drain on kitchen paper and serve with chutney or tomato sauce.

Curry Puffs

PREPARATION TIME: 1 hour
COOKING TIME: 20 minutes
SERVES: 4-6

450g (1lb) ready-made puff pastry

Filling

45ml (3 tblsp) oil
1 large onion, peeled and chopped
5ml (1 tsp) cumin seeds
450g (1lb) potatoes, peeled and diced
2 carrots, peeled and shredded
100g (4oz) shelled peas
5ml (1 tsp) salt
5ml (1 tsp) freshly ground black pepper
2-3 sprigs fresh green coriander leaves, chopped
5ml (1 tsp) garam masala powder

Flour paste: mix together 10ml (2 tsp) flour with water to make a sticky paste.

Heat the oil and fry the onion for 2 minutes. Add cumin seeds and allow to crackle, then add the diced potatoes. Stir fry over a medium heat for 5-6 minutes. Add the carrots and stir fry for 2 minutes. Add the peas and season with salt, pepper and chopped coriander leaves. Stir well. Cover and cook for 5-6 minutes or until the potatoes are tender. Sprinkle with the garam masala and lemon juice. Mix well. Remove from the heat and allow to cool. Roll out the puff pastry thinly. Cut into 7.5cm (3 inch) by 15cm (6 inch) rectangles. Place 15ml (1 tblsp) filling at one end and roll up the pastry like a swiss roll. Secure the ends with the

Potato Cutlets (top), Samosa (above left) and Curry Puffs (left).

Slice the tops off the tomatoes and scoop out the centre pulp, leaving a 2cm (¾ inch) "shell". Reserve the tomato pulp. Heat the oil in the frying pan and fry the onions for 2-3 minutes. Add the parsley, cooked rice, nuts, sesame seeds, salt and pepper and allspice. Add the tomato pulp and any juice which may have formed. Cook, uncovered, for 3-4 minutes, until most of the moisture has evaporated. Stuff the hollowed tomatoes with the rice mixture and arrange in a large frying pan. Add the stock and cook for 4 minutes. Remove the tomatoes. Bring the liquid back to the boil and add the blended cornflour and lemon juice. Remove from the heat. Add the beaten egg a little at a time. Return the mixture to the heat and cook until thickened. Add the stuffed tomatoes and cook over a low heat for 5 minutes, spooning the sauce over the tomatoes from time to time.

Fritters
(TEMPURA)

PREPARATION TIME: 10 minutes

COOKING TIME: 10-15 minutes

SERVES: 4 people

Batter
225g (8oz) plain flour
15ml (1 tblsp) cornflour
1.25ml (¼ tsp) salt
250ml (8 fl oz) chilled water
1 egg yolk
2 egg whites, stiffly beaten

Oil for deep frying
225g (8oz) fresh green beans, cut into 5cm (2 inch) pieces
10-12 fresh asparagus spears, cut in 5cm (2 inch) lengths
1 aubergine, cut into 2.5cm (1 inch) cubes
1 large potato, peeled and sliced 5mm (¼ inch) thick
10-12 fresh mushrooms, halved
6-8 cauliflower florets, halved

Tempura sauce: A
250ml (8 fl oz) water
60ml (2 fl oz) sherry
60ml (2 fl oz) soya sauce
5ml (1 tsp) sugar
½ a vegetable stock cube

Mix the ingredients together and bring to the boil. Stir until dissolved.

Tempura sauce: B
2.5cm (1 inch) fresh root ginger, peeled and grated
30ml (2 tblsp) grated turnip

30ml (2 tblsp) grated radish
45ml (3 tblsp) prepared mustard
45ml (3 tblsp) soya sauce

Mix the ingredients together and keep covered.

To make the batter: mix together the flour, cornflour and salt. Make a well in the centre. Mix the chilled water and egg yolk together and pour into the centre of the flour. Stir in the flour and blend lightly. Fold in the whisked egg whites.

Heat oil for deep frying. Dip the vegetables into the batter and fry in hot oil for 2-3 minutes until golden. Drain on kitchen paper and serve hot with the Tempura sauces. Use the batter within a few minutes of making. Do not allow it to stand for long.

Cheese and Lentil Rissoles

PREPARATION TIME: 30 minutes

COOKING TIME: 1 hour

SERVES: 4 people

175g (6oz) red lentils
400ml (⅔ pint) water
100g (4oz) grated cheese
1 medium onion, peeled and chopped
2 large eggs
50g (2oz) fresh breadcrumbs
5ml (1 tsp) mixed dried herbs
15ml (1 tblsp) lemon juice
Salt to taste
2.5ml (½ tsp) freshly ground black pepper
Oil for shallow frying

Wash the lentils in 3-4 changes of water. Drain the lentils and put them into a pan with the water. Cook until the lentils are tender and the water has been absorbed. Remove from heat and allow to cool. Mix the cooked lentils with the cheese, onion, egg, breadcrumbs, herbs, salt and pepper and the lemon juice. Mix well and shape into rissoles. Shallow fry the rissoles for 4-5 minutes on each side until golden brown. Drain on absorbent paper and serve immediately.

Mixed Nut Rissoles

PREPARATION TIME: 15 minutes

COOKING TIME: 20-25 minutes

SERVES: 4 people

25g (1oz) hazelnuts, chopped
50g (2oz) shelled peanuts, chopped
50g (2oz) cashew nuts, chopped

25g (1oz) pistachio nuts, chopped
1 onion, peeled and chopped
75g (3oz) fresh breadcrumbs
3 eggs, beaten
Salt and freshly ground black pepper to taste
2.5ml (½ tsp) dried, chopped marjoram
1 carrot, peeled and grated
15ml (1 tblsp) lemon juice
Little milk
Oil for shallow frying

Mix the chopped nuts with the onion, breadcrumbs, eggs, salt and pepper, marjoram, carrot and lemon juice. Add a little milk to bind the mixture, if necessary. Shape into rissoles. Shallow fry the rissoles in oil, for 4-5 minutes on each side, until golden brown. Drain well on absorbent paper and serve immediately. Alternatively, brush the rissoles generously with oil, put them onto a baking tray and bake in the oven at 220°C, 425°F, Gas Mark 7 for 15 minutes. Turn the rissoles halfway through cooking and brush with extra oil.

Cashew Nut Pie

PREPARATION TIME: 20-25 minutes

COOKING TIME: 30-40 minutes

SERVES: 4 people

Filling
2 medium onions, peeled and chopped
30ml (2 tblsp) oil
225g (8oz) shredded cabbage
50g (2oz) carrots, peeled and grated

Pie Crust
100g (4oz) crushed cornflakes
50g (2oz) cashew nuts, coarsely ground
175g (6oz) grated cheese
5ml (1 tsp) mixed dried herbs
Salt and freshly ground black pepper to taste
2 large eggs
100g (4oz) fresh breadcrumbs
15ml (1 tblsp) oil
50g (2oz) butter

To make the filling: fry the onions in the oil for 2 minutes; add the cabbage and carrots and fry for a further 4-5 minutes. Remove from the heat and allow to cool.

To make the pie crust: mix all the ingredients together in a bowl, apart from the oil, butter and 50g (2oz) of the grated cheese. Grease a baking tray with the oil. Press half the pie crust ingredients out to form an even base. Spread the filling mixture on top, and then press over the remaining pie crust

ingredients. Sprinkle with the remaining grated cheese and dot with butter. Bake in oven at 200°C, 400°F, Gas Mark 6, for 25-30 minutes.

Tomato, Onion and Mushroom Flan

PREPARATION TIME: 20 minutes

COOKING TIME: 40-45 minutes

SERVES: 6 people

225g (8oz) shortcrust pastry
225g (8oz) grated Cheddar cheese
4 tomatoes, skinned and chopped
15ml (1 tblsp) chopped chives or parsley
100g (4oz) mushrooms, sliced
10ml (2 tsp) corn oil
1 large onion, peeled and chopped
3 eggs, beaten
150ml (¼ pint) milk
2.5ml (½ tsp) salt
1.25ml (¼ tsp) freshly ground black pepper

Roll out the pastry and use to line a 20-23cm (8-9 inch) flan dish. Put 50g (2oz) of the grated cheese into the pastry case followed by the tomatoes, chives or parsley and the mushrooms. Heat the corn oil and fry the onion for 2-3 minutes. Mix the beaten eggs with the milk, salt and pepper and fried onion. Pour into the flan case and top with the remaining grated cheese. Bake at 200°C, 400°F Gas Mark 6 for 35-40 minutes, or until set. Serve hot or cold.

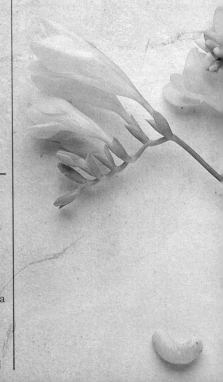

Mixed Nut Rissoles (left),
Cheese and Lentil Rissoles
(below) and Cashew Nut Pie
(bottom).

Pakora

This is the Indian version of vegetable fritters. Fried with or without batter, they make an interesting starter or snack.

PREPARATION TIME: 15 minutes

COOKING TIME: 15-20 minutes

SERVES: 4-6 people

1 large potato, or
2 medium potatoes, peeled and cut
   into 5mm (¼ inch) thick slices
8-10 cauliflower florets, halved
   lengthways
6 carrots, cut into 5cm (2 inch)
   lengths and halved
1 aubergine, cut into 5cm (2 inch)
   cubes
6 courgettes, trimmed and cut into
   5cm (2 inch) pieces and then
   quartered
1-2 green peppers, seeded and cut
   into 5mm (¼ inch) thick rounds or
   2.5cm (1 inch) pieces
5ml (1 tsp) salt
5ml (1 tsp) red chilli powder
2.5ml (½ tsp) turmeric powder
Oil for deep frying
6 lemon wedges

Sprinkle the vegetables with the spices and rub well in. Keep on one side. Heat the oil for deep frying. When it is beginning to smoke, reduce the heat. Fry the vegetables a few at a time, in batches. Fry for 2-3 minutes and drain on kitchen paper. Serve piping hot with wedges of lemon and a sweet and sour chutney or tomato ketchup. (These uncoated fritters are called Bhaja).

Batter
275g (10oz) baisen flour, sieved
5ml (1 tsp) salt
5ml (1 tsp) chilli powder
5ml (1 tsp) ground cumin
15ml (1 tblsp) lemon juice
300ml (½ pint) water

Mix the sieved flour with the salt, chilli powder, cumin and lemon juice. Make a well in the centre and add the water; stir in the baisen flour until all the flour has been incorporated. Beat well to give a smooth batter. Adjust seasoning. Allow the batter to stand for a few minutes. Heat the oil as above. Dip the vegetables into the batter and then fry for 2-3 minutes. Drain on kitchen paper and serve piping hot with tomato sauce. Other vegetables which may be used: onions rings, raw banana slices, green tomato slices, spinach leaves.

Stuffed Mushrooms

PREPARATION TIME: 20 minutes

COOKING TIME: 10-15 minutes

SERVES: 4-6 people

Filling
1 small onion, peeled and finely
   chopped
10ml (2 tsp) oil
1cm (½ inch) fresh root ginger, peeled
   and crushed
2 cloves garlic, peeled and crushed
225g (8oz) boiled, peeled and
   mashed potatoes
Salt and freshly ground black pepper
   to taste
15ml (1 tblsp) lemon juice
10ml (2 tsp) chopped chives or
   parsley
20-24 large button mushrooms
175g (6oz) grated Cheddar cheese
Oil for brushing

Fry the onion in the 10ml (2 tsp) oil for 2 minutes; add the ginger and garlic. Fry for 1 minute and mix with the mashed potatoes. Season to taste with salt, pepper, lemon juice and chopped parsley. Mix well. Remove the stalks from the mushrooms; stuff the hollows with the potato filling and top with a little Cheddar cheese. Brush the mushrooms with a little oil and arrange them on a baking tray. Bake the mushrooms in a moderately hot oven, 190°C, 375°F, Gas Mark 5, for 10 minutes until the cheese is brown.

Aloo Bonda

This is an Indian potato fritter recipe made in the shape of spicy balls. Eaten hot or cold, they are ideal for parties, snacks and picnics.

PREPARATION TIME: 25 minutes

COOKING TIME: 30 minutes

SERVES: 4-6 people

Batter
225g (8oz) baisen flour, sieved
1.25ml (¼ tsp) salt
1.25ml (¼ tsp) baking powder
300ml (½ pint) water

450g (1lb) potatoes, boiled in their
   skins and peeled
1 large or 2 medium onions, peeled
   and chopped
2.5cm (1 inch) fresh root ginger,
   peeled and finely chopped
2-3 green chillies, chopped
4-5 sprigs fresh green coriander
   leaves, chopped
2.5ml (½ tsp) salt
1.25ml (¼ tsp) freshly ground black
   pepper
15ml (1 tblsp) lemon juice
Oil for deep frying

Mix the sieved flour with the salt and baking powder. Make a well in the centre and add the water. Beat well to give a smooth batter. Chop the boiled potatoes into tiny cubes; add the chopped onions, ginger, chillies, coriander leaves, salt and pepper to taste and lemon juice. Mix well and adjust seasoning to taste. Mould into even-sized balls with dampened hands. Heat the oil for deep frying. When hot, dip the vegetable balls into the batter and then fry for 3-4 minutes over a gentle heat until golden brown. Drain on kitchen paper and serve with tomato sauce.

This page: Aloo Bonda (top), Fritters (Tempura) (centre right) and Pakora (bottom left).

Facing page: Stuffed Tomatoes (top right), Stuffed Mushrooms (centre left) and Tomato, Onion and Mushroom Flan (bottom).

Salads

Onion Salad

This salad is usually served as an accompaniment to kebabs. Onion salad goes very well with a variety of main courses, as a side salad.

PREPARATION TIME: 5-7 minutes
SERVES: 4 people

2 large Spanish onions, peeled and thinly sliced
2-3 sprigs fresh green coriander, chopped
1 green chilli, sliced
Juice of 1 lemon
2.5ml (½ tsp) salt
Pinch paprika

Combine the onion rings, coriander leaves and chilli in a bowl. Add the lemon juice and salt and mix well. Put the onion salad onto a serving plate and sprinkle with paprika.

Tabbouleh

This is a Lebanese salad and it is very good for parties and picnics.

PREPARATION TIME: 2 hours 30 minutes
SERVES: 6 people

225g (8oz) bulgar or pourgouri (precooked, cracked wheat)
250ml (8 fl oz) boiling water
8-10 spring onions, chopped
1 green pepper, seeded and chopped
120ml (8 tblsp) chopped parsley
30ml (2 tblsp) chopped mint leaves

Dressing
45ml (3 tblsp) lemon juice
175ml (6 fl oz) olive oil
5ml (1 tsp) grated lemon peel
5ml (1 tsp) ground mixed spice
2.5ml (½ tsp) ground cumin
5ml (1 tsp) salt
1.25ml (¼ tsp) freshly ground black pepper
1 small iceberg lettuce, shredded
2 large firm tomatoes, cut into wedges
10-15 pitted black olives, halved
2-3 sprigs mint
1-2 sprigs fresh green coriander

Place the pourgouri or bulgar into a bowl and add boiling water. Cover and stand for 1½-2 hours. Drain the bulgar by squeezing out the excess water. Mix the spring onions, green pepper, parsley and mint with the bulgar. Combine all the dressing ingredients in a screw top jar and shake well. Pour the dressing over the bulgar mixture and mix lightly. Line a platter with shredded lettuce. Place the prepared bulgar in the centre. Garnish with tomato, olives, mint and coriander leaves.

Sweet and Sour Coleslaw

A variation on the usual theme, but a definite winner.

PREPARATION TIME: 20 minutes
SERVES: 6 people

½ small red cabbage, shredded
1 small green cabbage, shredded
1 large sweet carrot, peeled and shredded
3 spring onions, finely chopped
75ml (5 tblsp) cider vinegar
45ml (3 tblsp) brown sugar
2.5ml (½ tsp) salt
1.25ml (¼ tsp) freshly ground black pepper
75ml (5 tblsp) soured cream
5ml (1 tsp) French mustard

Combine the red and green cabbage, carrots and spring onions in a mixing bowl. Mix the vinegar, sugar and salt and pepper in a small saucepan and stir over the heat to dissolve the sugar. Pour the hot vinegar sauce over the cabbage mixture and mix well. Stir the soured cream and mustard together in a separate bowl; stir this mixture into the vegetables. Mix well and serve.

Mixed Bean Salad

This nutritious salad is made from a medley of beans and is very good for health conscious and athletic people. Either cook the dried beans at home or buy ready-cooked ones. Soak the beans separately overnight, and then boil them separately until tender. Drain well.

PREPARATION TIME: 15 minutes
SERVES: 4-6 people

175g (6oz) cooked red kidney beans
175g (6oz) cooked black eyed beans (Lobia)
175g (6oz) cooked chick peas
175g (6oz) cooked butter beans
100g (4oz) shelled broad beans
225g (8oz) sliced green beans, blanched

Dressing
30ml (2 tblsp) brown sugar
120ml (4 fl oz) white wine vinegar
2.5ml (½ tsp) salt
1.25ml (¼ tsp) freshly ground black pepper
120ml (4 fl oz) olive oil
2.5ml (½ tsp) dry mustard powder
2.5ml (½ tsp) dried basil leaves
1 large Spanish or red onion, peeled and thinly sliced into rings
30ml (2 tblsp) chopped parsley

Mix all the beans together in a large bowl. Mix the sugar and vinegar together with salt and pepper to taste. Stir in the oil, mustard and basil. Pour this vinegar mixture over the beans. Mix thoroughly. Refrigerate until ready to serve. Before serving, mix in the onion rings and parsley.

Nutty Salad

PREPARATION TIME: 20 minutes
SERVES: 4 people

450g (1lb) boiled potatoes, diced
175g (6oz) shelled green peas
100g (4oz) cooked carrots, diced
1 medium onion, peeled and chopped
1 small green pepper, seeded and chopped
8-10 radishes, chopped
2 stems celery, chopped
¼ cucumber, chopped
50g (2oz) roasted peanuts, coarsely chopped
50g (2oz) grated fresh coconut
15ml (1 tblsp) sunflower seeds
2-3 sprigs fresh green coriander leaves or parsley, chopped

Dressing
30ml (2 tblsp) lemon juice
60ml (4 tblsp) olive oil
5ml (1 tsp) salt
2.5ml (½ tsp) freshly ground black pepper
2.5ml (½ tsp) brown sugar

Mix all the vegetables together, except the nuts and sunflower seeds, in a large bowl. Mix the dressing ingredients together in a screw top jar and shake well. Add the dressing to the salad and mix throughly. Sprinkle with the nuts and sunflower seeds before serving.

Rice and Nut Salad

This salad has a very refreshing taste. The main ingredients are nuts, raisins, carrots and rice.

PREPARATION TIME: 15 minutes
SERVES: 4 people

30ml (2 tblsp) olive oil
30ml (2 tblsp) lemon juice
Salt and freshly ground black pepper to taste
100g (4oz) sultanas
50g (2oz) currants
275g (10oz) cooked long grain rice, well drained
75g (3oz) chopped blanched almonds
50g (2oz) cashew nuts, chopped
50g (2oz) shelled walnuts, chopped
425g (15oz) can peach slices, drained and chopped
¼ cucumber, cubed
100g (4oz) cooked red kidney beans
15ml (1 tblsp) chopped pitted olives

Mix the olive oil, lemon juice and salt and freshly ground black pepper in a screw top jar; shake vigorously. Soak the sultanas and

Facing page: Onion Salad (top), Nutty Salad (centre) and Tabbouleh (bottom).

currants in sufficient boiling water to cover, for 10 minutes. Drain the fruits. Mix the rice, nuts and soaked sultanas and currants. Add the chopped peaches, cucumber, red kidney beans and olives. Pour the dressing over the salad and toss lightly together. Serve on a bed of chopped lettuce.

Cheese Salad

This cheese salad originates from Greece and has many variations; it is popularly known as Horiatiki.

PREPARATION TIME: 10-12 minutes

SERVES: 4 people

½ a head of endive
½ iceberg lettuce
1 cucumber, peeled and sliced
3-4 large tomatoes, cut into wedges, or
15-20 cherry tomatoes, halved
8-10 pitted green or black olives, halved
1 medium Spanish or red onion, peeled and chopped
125g (4oz) Feta cheese, cut into 1cm (½ inch) pieces

Dressing

75ml (5 tblsp) olive oil
30ml (2 tblsp) red wine vinegar
5ml (1 tsp) chopped fresh oregano or
1.25ml (¼ tsp) dried oregano
2.5ml (½ tsp) salt
1.25ml (¼ tsp) freshly ground black pepper
2.5ml (½ tsp) brown sugar

Wash and dry the endive and lettuce leaves; tear into bite size pieces. Place the endive and lettuce in a large bowl and add the cucumber, tomatoes, olives, onion and cheese. Shake the dressing

Cheese Salad (bottom left), Mixed Bean Salad (below) and Rice and Nut Salad (bottom right).

ingredients together in a screw top jar. Pour the dressing over the salad. Toss lightly and serve.

Mixed Fresh Vegetable Salad

This salad can be prepared with any combination of vegetables, in any proportion. Add or subtract according to personal taste.

PREPARATION TIME: 20 minutes
SERVES: 6 people

1 large spring onion, peeled and chopped
½ cucumber, diced
3 carrots, peeled and diced
6 large tomatoes, diced, or
8 cherry tomatoes, halved
10 button mushrooms, diced
3 stems celery, diced
1 green pepper, seeded and diced
15-20 tiny cauliflower florets
15-20 radishes, quartered
15ml (1 tblsp) chopped watercress or mustard and cress
2 sprigs fresh green coriander leaves or parsley, chopped

Dressing
2.5ml (½ tsp) salt
2.5ml (½ tsp) freshly ground black pepper
5ml (1 tsp) brown sugar
30ml (2 tblsp) cider vinegar
15ml (1 tblsp) lemon juice
15ml (1 tblsp) honey
60ml (4 tblsp) olive oil
Pinch mustard powder
8 lettuce leaves

Combine all the vegetables in a large bowl. Mix together all the dressing ingredients. Pour the dressing over the vegetables and serve on a bed of lettuce leaves.

Pasta Salad

This is a popular salad from America. It can be eaten as a main dish or as a side salad – it is a wonderful combination of vegetables, pasta and kidney beans.

PREPARATION TIME: 15-20 minutes

SERVES: 6 people

450g (1lb) cooked red kidney beans, drained
350g (12oz) pasta shells or spirals, cooked
1 large green pepper, seeded and sliced into 2.5cm (1 inch) long pieces
1 large red pepper, seeded and sliced into 2.5cm (1 inch) long pieces
20-30 pitted black olives, sliced in half
15ml (1 tblsp) capers
4-5 sprigs fresh parsley, chopped

Dressing

200ml (⅓ pint) olive oil
45ml (3 tblsp) lemon juice
10ml (2 tsp) finely chopped fresh basil leaves
5ml (1 tsp) salt
1.25ml (¼ tsp) freshly ground black pepper
2 cloves garlic, peeled and minced
1 small head curly endive

Combine the beans, pasta, peppers, olives, capers and parsley in a large bowl. Mix all the dressing ingredients together; add to the salad ingredients and toss together. Line the serving platter or bowl with endive leaves; place the pasta salad in the centre.

This page: Sweet and Sour Coleslaw (top left), Mixed Fresh Vegetable Salad (top right) and Pasta Salad (bottom).

Facing page: Kedgeree (top left), Sweet Savoury Rice (centre right) and Vegetable Pulao Rice (bottom).

Rice and Pulses

Kedgeree

PREPARATION TIME: 15 minutes, plus soaking time	
COOKING TIME: 30 minutes	
SERVES: 4-6 people	

225g (8oz) long grain rice
225g (8oz) red lentils
750ml (1¼ pints) tepid water
100g (4oz) butter (or an equivalent
  amount of olive oil)
1 medium onion, peeled and chopped
2.5ml (½ tsp) crushed fresh root
  ginger
2.5ml (½ tsp) crushed garlic
2.5cm (1 inch) piece cinnamon stick
6 cloves
1 bayleaf
5ml (1 tsp) ground coriander
1.25ml (¼ tsp) ground turmeric
2.5ml (½ tsp) salt
2 green chillies, sliced in half
  lengthways

Wash the rice and the lentils in 4 to 5 changes of water; soak them in the 750ml (1¼ pints) tepid water for 30 minutes. Heat the butter or oil in a large pan; add the onion and fry for 2-3 minutes. Add the ginger, garlic, cinnamon stick, cloves and bayleaf, and fry for 1 minute. Drain the water from the rice and lentils; reserve the water. Add the rice and lentils to the fried onion, together with the coriander, turmeric, slt and green chillies. Stir over the heat for 2-3 minutes, until the rice and lentils are evenly coated with fat. Add the reserved water and bring to the boil; reduce the heat and simmer covered for 8-10 minutes, without stirring, until the water has been absorbed and the rice and lentils are tender. Serve with a vegetable curry.

Vegetable Pulao Rice

PREPARATION TIME: 30 minutes	
COOKING TIME: 30 minutes	
SERVES: 4-6 people	

450g (1lb) long grain rice (Basmati)
750-900ml (1¼-1½ pints) water
1 medium onion, peeled and diced
2.5cm (1 inch) piece cinnamon stick
1 bayleaf

6 cloves
5ml (1 tsp) black cumin (shah-zeera)
6 small cardamoms
2.5ml (½ tsp) crushed fresh root
    ginger
2.5ml (½ tsp) crushed garlic
1 medium potato, peeled and diced
1 carrot, peeled and diced
100g (4oz) shelled peas
75g (3oz) sliced green beans
5ml (1 tsp) garam masala powder
2.5ml (½ tsp) chilli powder
5ml (1 tsp) ground coriander
5ml (1 tsp) ground cumin
5ml (1 tsp) salt
30ml (2 tblsp) lemon juice
100g (4oz) butter (or an equivalent
    amount of olive oil)

Wash the rice in 4-5 changes of water and soak in the 750-900ml (1¼-1½ pints) water for 30 minutes. Melt the butter in a pan and fry the onion for 2-3 minutes. Add the cinnamon, bayleaf, cloves, black cumin, cardamoms, ginger and garlic. Fry for 1 minute, stirring, and add the potato, carrot, peas, green beans, garam masala, chilli, coriander, cumin and salt. Mix well. Drain the soaked rice, retaining the water and add the rice to the onion and spices. Stir the mixture gently and add the reserved water. Bring to the boil and then reduce the heat; cover and simmer gently for 10-15 minutes, until the rice is tender and the water has been absorbed. Do not stir during cooking. Sprinkle with the lemon juice and serve. To colour pulao: dissolve a pinch of saffron in 15ml (1 tblsp) warm milk; pour over the rice and allow to stand over a very low heat for 5 minutes.

Mixed Daal

This is a mixed lentil stew, using 3 or 4 varieties of daal. Add a few vegetables of your choice to turn it into a substantial meal.

PREPARATION TIME: 15 minutes
COOKING TIME: 30 minutes
SERVES: 4 people

75g (3oz) split Bengal grain
    (Channa)
50g (2oz) yellow lentils (Toor Daal)
100g (4oz) red lentils (Masoor)
50g (2oz) dehusked split mung
    (Moong), or any other daal
2.5ml (½ tsp) ground turmeric
7.5ml (1½ tsp) ground coriander
4 canned tomatoes, chopped
2 green chillies

3 sprigs fresh green coriander leaves
Salt to taste
100g (4oz) butter
1cm (½ inch) fresh root ginger, peeled
    and chopped
1 onion, chopped
1 clove garlic, chopped

As some of these pulses have different cooking times, wash each pulse separately in 3-4 changes of water. Drain. Soak separately in water for 5 minutes. Bring 600ml (1 pint) water to the boil; add the drained channa daal. Boil for 15-20 minutes or until the pulses are tender. Add the remaining pulses well drained, and simmer gently with the turmeric and ground coriander for 15-20 minutes, or until all the pulses are soft. Beat with an egg whisk. Add the tomatoes, green chillies and coriander leaves. Simmer for a further 5-6 minutes. Pour into a serving bowl and keep warm. Melt the butter in a frying pan and fry the ginger for 2 minutes. Add the onion and garlic and fry until golden brown. Pour this mixture over the mixed daal and serve immediately.

Sweet Savoury Rice

PREPARATION TIME: 20 minutes
COOKING TIME: 30 minutes
SERVES: 4-6 people

450g (1lb) rice (Basmati or long
    grain)
750-900ml (1¼-1½ pints) water
50g (2oz) raisins
75g (3oz) cashew nuts, chopped
50g (2oz) blanched almonds, split
50g (2oz) pistachio nuts, split
100g (4oz) butter (or an equivalent
    amount of olive oil)
2.5cm (1 inch) piece cinnamon stick
6 cloves
6 small cardamoms
1 bayleaf
2.5cm (½ tsp) black cumin seed
    (shah-zeera)
100g (4oz) sultanas
5ml (1 tsp) salt
5ml (1 tsp) sugar
Pinch of saffron

Wash the rice in 4-5 changes of water and soak in the 750-900ml (1¼-1½ pints) water for 30 minutes. Soak the raisins and nuts in a little water for 10 minutes. Drain the raisins and nuts. Melt the butter in a large pan and fry the cinnamon, cloves, small

cardamoms, bayleaf and black cumin for 1-2 minutes. Add the nuts, raisins and sultanas. Drain the soaked rice retaining the water; add the rice to the saucepan. Fry for 1 minute. Add salt, sugar and the reserved water. Bring to the boil. Reduce the heat and add a pinch of saffron. Stir once gently. Cover and simmer gently for 10-15 minutes, without stirring, until the rice is tender and the water has been absorbed. Serve with curries.

Red Kidney Bean Curry

A popular dish from the Punjab province of India. It is similar to Chilli Con-Carne and makes a hearty meal with bread or rice.

PREPARATION TIME: overnight, plus 15 minutes
COOKING TIME: 20-45 minutes
SERVES: 4 people

225g (8oz) dried red kidney beans,
    washed and soaked overnight in
    sufficient water to cover
2 medium onions, chopped
45ml (3 tblsp) oil
1 bayleaf
2.5cm (1 inch) piece cinnamon stick
6 cloves
6 small green cardamoms
2 green chillies, quartered
3 cloves garlic, peeled and finely
    chopped
2.5cm (1 inch) fresh root ginger,
    peeled and finely chopped
2.5ml (½ tsp) chilli powder
1.25ml (¼ tsp) ground turmeric
7.5ml (1½ tsp) ground coriander
5ml (1 tsp) ground cumin
5ml (1 tsp) garam masala powder
425g (15oz) can peeled tomatoes,
    chopped
2.5ml (½ tsp) salt
2-3 sprigs fresh green coriander,
    chopped

Either pressure cook the red kidney beans for 5-6 minutes, or cook them in their soaking water for 15-20 minutes until soft. Remove from the heat; allow to stand, covered. Fry the onions in the oil in a large saucepan over a moderate heat until tender. Add the bayleaf, cinnamon, cloves and cardamoms and fry for 1 minute. Add the chillies, garlic and ginger and fry until golden. Sprinkle with the chilli powder, turmeric, ground coriander, ground cumin and garam masala. Avoid burning the mixture. Stir the mixture to blend the spices. Add the tomatoes and

season with salt. Cover and simmer for 2-3 minutes. Drain the cooked beans and collect the thick red liquid. Add the beans to the spiced tomato mixture. Stir gently and cook for 1 minute. Add the red liquid and chopped coriander; cover and simmer for 3-5 minutes. Serve with bread or boiled rice.

Red Lentil Daal

There is an abundance of natural protein in pulses and there is a great variety of pulses now available.

PREPARATION TIME: 10 minutes
COOKING TIME: 30 minutes
SERVES: 4 people

225g (8oz) red lentils
350ml (12 fl oz) water
1.25ml (¼ tsp) ground turmeric
5ml (1 tsp) ground coriander
1 green chilli, cut in half
Salt to taste
4-6 canned tomatoes, chopped
2 sprigs fresh green coriander leaves,
    chopped
50g (2oz) butter
1 small onion, peeled and finely
    chopped

Wash the lentils in 3-5 changes of water. Put the lentils into a pan with the 350ml (12 fl oz) water; cover and cook over a low heat for 10-15 minutes. Remove any froth with a spoon. Once the lentils are tender and yellow, blend until smooth with an egg whisk. Add the turmeric, ground coriander, chilli, salt to taste and chopped tomatoes. Cover and simmer for 10 minutes. Add the coriander leaves and pour into a dish. Keep warm. Melt the butter in a frying pan and saute the onion until golden brown. Pour the onions and butter juices over the daal. Serve with rice or bread.

Facing page: Mixed Daal (top left), Red Kidney Bean Curry (centre) and Red Lentil Daal (bottom).

Bread and Pizza

Puri

These deep-fried breads are simple to make once the art has been mastered.

PREPARATION TIME:	10-15 minutes
COOKING TIME:	20 minutes
MAKES:	30-32

450g (1lb) wholemeal flour
2.5ml (½ tsp) salt
250-300ml (8-12 fl oz) water
Oil for deep frying

Sieve the flour and salt into a mixing bowl. Mix to a soft dough with water. Knead well and leave to relax for 5 minutes, covered with a damp cloth. Divide the dough into 30-32 small even sized balls; roll out each ball into a small round about 6-7cm (2½-3 inch) in diameter. Heat the oil for deep frying and drop in a small piece of dough. If it rises to the top instantly then the correct temperature for frying has been reached. Place one puri at a time into the hot oil, taking care not to splash the oil. Gently stir the puri and it will begin to swell. Turn over and cook on the underside until golden brown – about ½-1 minute. The flip side is always the thick side and it needs extra cooking time. Drain the puris on the side of the frying pan, and place them on

Puri (above), Roti (right) and Paratha (far right).

kitchen paper to drain, before serving. Puris are best when served piping hot. Puris can be served cold and they can also be reheated under the grill.

Paratha

These shallow-fried breads can either be made plain, or stuffed with a favourite filling, such as cheese, potato etc.

PREPARATION TIME:	15-20 minutes
COOKING TIME:	20-30 minutes
MAKES:	16-18

450g (1lb) wholemeal flour
2.5ml (½ tsp) salt
250-300ml (8-12 fl oz) water
Melted butter or oil

Sieve the flour and salt into a mixing bowl. Mix to a soft dough with water. Knead the dough well; leave to relax, covered, for 5 minutes. Divide the dough into 16-18 even-sized balls. Roll each ball into a small round about 5cm (2 inches) in diameter. Brush each round of dough with oil or melted butter and fold in half. Brush the upper folded surface with oil or butter and fold in half to form a small triangle. On a well floured surface roll out these triangles thinly. Heat a solid based frying pan or a griddle. Put the paratha onto the heated frying pan and cook for ½-1 minute or until small brown specks appear. Cook the other side in the same way. Brush a little oil or butter over the paratha and turn over. Fry for 1 minute and then brush the second side with oil or butter. Fry on both sides until the

paratha is golden and crisp. Make the rest of the paratha in the same way. Keep them soft and warm, well wrapped in a clean tea towel or foil.

Roti

Roti is best made with wholemeal flour; any variety may be used.

PREPARATION TIME: 20 minutes

COOKING TIME: 20-30 minutes

MAKES: about 24

450g (1lb) wholemeal flour
2.5ml (½ tsp) salt
250-300ml (8-12 fl oz) water

Sieve the flour and salt into a mixing bowl. Mix to a soft dough with water. Knead the dough for 2-3 minutes. Cover and allow to relax for 5-6 minutes before shaping the bread. Divide the dough into 25g (1oz) balls. Roll each ball into a thin round about 13-15cm (5-6 inches) in diameter. Place a solid based frying pan or a griddle over a medium heat; when the pan is hot, place the shaped roti onto it. Cook for ½ minute on each side and then place under a preheated grill to bloat (little brown specks will appear on the surface). The first 2 rotis do not usually bloat, so do not be alarmed. Make all the rotis and stack them one on top of each other. Keep them covered with a clean tea towel or foil. Serve hot with any curry or spicy savoury dish.

Banana and Nut Bread

PREPARATION TIME: 30 minutes

COOKING TIME: 1 hour

MAKES: 1 loaf

100g (4oz) butter
225g (8oz) brown sugar
1 egg, well beaten
225g (8oz) wholemeal flour
2.5ml (½ tsp) salt
7.5ml (1½ tsp) baking powder
60ml (4 tblsp) natural yogurt
2 ripe bananas, peeled and mashed
50g (2oz) raisins
100g (4oz) mixed nuts, chopped

Preheat the oven to 180°C, 350°F, Gas Mark 4. Cream the butter and sugar until light and fluffy and gradually beat in the egg. Sieve the flour, salt and baking powder together. Add half the yogurt to the butter and sugar mixture and then mix in half the sieved dry ingredients. Beat in the remaining yogurt, flour, mashed banana, raisins and chopped nuts. Mix well. Put the mixture into a greased loaf tin. Bake at 180°C, 350°F, Gas Mark 4, for 1 hour.

Crusty Loaf

PREPARATION TIME: 3 hours 40 minutes

COOKING TIME: 45 minutes-1 hour

MAKES: 2 loaves

300ml (½ pint) tepid water
15g (½oz) fresh yeast or 10ml (2 tsp) dried yeast
2.5ml (½ tsp) salt
15g (½oz) butter
15ml (1 tblsp) sugar
400g (14oz) sieved plain flour
15ml (1 tblsp) melted butter
25g (1oz) caraway, sesame or poppy seeds for topping (optional)

Sprinkle or crumble the yeast into the tepid water; stir to dissolve. Leave for a few minutes until frothy. Mix the salt, butter, sugar and flour together; stir in the yeast liquid and mix to a dough. Knead the dough for 10 minutes on a lightly floured surface. Place the dough in a greased bowl and brush the top lightly with melted butter; cover with a damp cloth and leave it to rise in a warm place (free from draught), until doubled in bulk (about 40-45 minutes). Punch the dough down and let it rise again until almost double its original size about (30 minutes). Punch down once again and turn out onto a floured surface, cut into two equal portions. Roll each one into an oblong about 20-25cm (8-10 inches) in length. Beginning with the wide side, roll up each oblong tightly. Seal the edges by pinching together. Holding each end of the roll, roll it gently backwards and forwards to lengthen the loaf and shape the ends. Place the loaves on a greased baking sheet lightly sprinkled with plain flour. Brush the loaves either with milk, or with cornflour glaze, and leave to rise for 1½ hours, uncovered. With a sharp knife, make 5mm (¼ inch) slashes at regular intervals. Bake in a hot oven, 200°C, 400°F, Gas Mark 6, for 10 minutes. Brush once again with milk or cornflour glaze and sprinkle with poppy seeds (or other seeds). Return to the oven and bake for 25-30 minutes or until golden brown.

To make cornflour glaze: mix 5ml (1 tsp) cornflour with 5ml (1 tsp) cold water. Add 120ml (4oz) boiling water and cook for 1-2 minutes until smooth. Cool slightly before use.

Wholemeal Bread

PREPARATION TIME: 2 hours 30 minutes

COOKING TIME: 50 minutes

MAKES: 1 large loaf

750g (1½lbs) wholemeal flour
2.5ml (½ tsp) salt
50g (2oz) margarine
25g (1oz) fresh yeast, or
15ml (1 tblsp) dried yeast (see below)
15ml (1 tblsp) granulated or brown sugar
300ml (½ pint) tepid water
150ml (¼ pint) tepid milk
15ml (1 tblsp) melted butter

Sieve the flour and salt into a warm bowl and rub in the margarine. Cream the fresh yeast with the sugar and stir in the warm water and milk. (If using dried yeast, sprinkle it onto the warm water and milk, with the sugar, and leave to stand for 10 minutes until thick and frothy). Make a well in the centre of the flour and pour in the yeast liquid; gradually mix in the flour to form a dough. Knead the dough well. Cover it with a damp cloth and leave to rise until double in bulk (about 1¼ hours). Grease a loaf tin, 23cm by 13cm by 7.5cm (9 inches by 5 inches by 3 inches). Turn the risen dough onto a floured surface and knead well; place in the loaf tin. Leave in a warm place to rise for 40 minutes. Brush the loaf with melted butter and bake at 200°C, 400°F, Gas Mark 6, for about 50 minutes

Wholemeal Pizza Dough

PREPARATION TIME: 50-60 minutes

200ml (⅓ pint) tepid water
7.5ml (1½ tsp) dried yeast
2.5ml (½ tsp) salt
5ml (1 tsp) sugar
5ml (1 tsp) olive oil
100g (4oz) wholemeal flour
150g (5oz) plain flour

Mix the dried yeast with the tepid water. Add the salt, sugar and oil. Mix in the flours a little at a time, to make a dough. Use extra water if needed. Turn the dough onto a lightly floured surface and knead until smooth (about 5-8 minutes). Cover the dough with a clean damp tea towel and leave to stand for 15-20 minutes. Knead once more for 1-2 minutes. You can make either one large pizza base or several smaller ones. Grease one 35cm (14 inch) pizza pan and roll out the dough to make a round large enough to fit the pizza pan. Shape the pizza dough with the hands to fit the pan. Top with the chosen topping and bake.

Basic Pizza Dough

This is the basic recipe for pizza dough and although there are many variations, the making of the dough is very important. Pizza originated in Italy, around the Naples area, but it is now eaten and enjoyed worldwide. Once the basic dough is perfected, toppings can be adjusted to one's taste. In fact, on one single pizza, each slice can have a different taste (i.e. with a different topping). See Taco Pizza Topping and Mixed Vegetable Pizza Topping recipes.

PREPARATION TIME: about 1 hour 30 minutes

1.25ml (¼ tsp) sugar
15ml (1 tblsp) dried yeast
120ml (4 fl oz) tepid water
5ml (1 tsp) salt
225g (8oz) plain flour, sieved

Mix the dried yeast with 30ml (2 tblsp) of the tepid water and the sugar. Stir until dissolved. Leave to stand for 10-15 minutes until frothy. Put the flour and salt into a

Facing page: Crusty Loaf (top), Banana and Nut Bread (centre) and Wholemeal Bread (bottom).

bowl and make a well in the centre. Add the yeast liquid and the remaining tepid water; mix to form a dough. Knead the dough on a floured surface for 8-10 minutes. Cover with a damp cloth and leave to rise in a warm place for 40-45 minutes, until double its original size. Knead once again on a lightly floured surface for 3-5 minutes until soft and elastic. You can make either one large pizza base, or several smaller ones. Grease one 35cm (14 inch) pizza pan and roll out the dough. Shape the pizza dough with the hands to fit the pan. Top with the chosen topping and bake.

Taco Pizza

This idea is taken from the taco (a Mexican pancake). The pizza base is made with a mixture of cornmeal and flour and some of the topping ingredients are the same as those used in a taco filling.

PREPARATION TIME: 30-40 minutes

COOKING TIME: 30-35 minutes

SERVES: 6 people

Dough

175g (6oz) plain flour
75g (3oz) fine yellow cornmeal
10ml (2 tsp) baking powder
5ml (1 tsp) salt
100g (4oz) margarine
120ml (4 fl oz) milk

Sieve the flour, cornmeal, salt and baking powder into a mixing bowl. Rub in the margarine. Add the milk, gradually, to form a medium soft dough. Knead the dough on a well floured surface for 4-5 minutes, until smooth. Roll into a circle to cover a 33-35cm (13-14 inch) pizza pan, with a 2.5cm (1 inch) high rim. Grease the pizza pan and cover with the dough. Shape the pizza dough to fit the pan. Pinch the edges to form a deep rim. Keep on one side until the topping is ready.

Topping
30ml (2 tblsp) olive oil
1 clove garlic, peeled and crushed
1 small onion, peeled and chopped
½ green pepper, seeded and coarsely chopped
4-6 mushrooms, sliced
225g (8oz) cooked red kidney beans (or drained canned ones)
2 spring onions, chopped
3 large tomatoes, chopped
6-8 pitted black olives, halved
3-4 pickled Mexican chillies, chopped
225g (8oz) Mozzarella, Cheddar or Monterey Jack cheese, cut into slivers
1 carrot, peeled and grated
150ml (¼ pint) soured cream
Bottled taco sauce

Heat the oil and fry the garlic, chopped onion, pepper and mushrooms for 2 minutes; add the kidney beans and stir fry for 1-2 minutes. Remove from the heat and stir in the spring onions. Spread the above topping mixture over the pizza base. Arrange the tomatoes evenly on top. Add the olives, Mexican chillies and slivers of cheese. Bake at 200°C, 400°F, Gas mark 6, for 15-20 minutes until the edges turn golden brown and crusty. Serve with grated carrots, whipped soured cream and taco sauce.

Mixed Vegetable Pizza Topping

PREPARATION TIME: 30 minutes

COOKING TIME: 20 minutes

SERVES: 4-6 people

30ml (2 tblsp) olive oil
1 small onion, peeled and chopped
2 spring onions, chopped
1 medium courgette, trimmed and thinly sliced
4 mushrooms, sliced
Salt and freshly ground black pepper to taste
6-8 canned tomatoes, chopped
10ml (2 tsp) tomato puree

8 pitted black olives
2 tomatoes, thinly sliced
1 green pepper, seeded and chopped
1 green chilli, chopped
5ml (1 tsp) dried oregano
175g (6oz) Mozzarella cheese, Cheddar cheese or a mixture of the two, cut into thin slivers
30ml (2 tblsp) grated Parmesan cheese

Heat the olive oil in a large frying pan; add the onions and sauté for 1-2 minutes. Add the courgette and sauté for 2 minutes. Add the mushrooms and salt and pepper to taste and stir fry for 1 minute to glaze the vegetables. Remove from the heat and cool. Mix the chopped tomato with the tomato puree and spread evenly over the pizza base. Spoon the vegetable mixture over the pizza and arrange the olives, sliced tomatoes, green pepper and green chilli on top. Sprinkle with the oregano, the slivers of cheese and the grated Parmesan cheese. Bake at 230°C, 450°F, Gas mark 8 for 12-15 minutes, or until the edge of the pizza is golden brown and crusty.

Taco Pizza (top right) and Mixed Vegetable Pizza Topping (bottom right).

Main Meals

Okra Curry

A dry vegetable curry made with okra and potato.

PREPARATION TIME: 10-15 minutes

COOKING TIME: 30 minutes

SERVES: 4 people

45ml (3 tblsp) oil
1 onion, peeled and chopped
2 medium sized potatoes, peeled and cut into 2.5cm (1 inch) pieces
450g (1lb) okra, topped and tailed, and chopped into 1cm (½ inch) pieces
Salt to taste
2.5ml (½ tsp) ground turmeric
5ml (1 tsp) chilli powder
7.5ml (1½ tsp) ground coriander
2-3 sprigs fresh green coriander leaves, chopped

Heat the oil in a wok or solid based frying pan and fry the onion for 3-4 minutes. Stir in the cubed potatoes; cover and cook for 3-4 minutes. Add the okra, and stir fry for 2 minutes. Sprinkle with salt to taste, turmeric, chilli and ground coriander. Mix gently; cover and cook for 8-10 minutes. Stir occasionally and continue cooking until the potatoes are tender. Sprinkle with the chopped coriander leaves. Mix well and serve.

Okra Fry

This is a dry "curry" – no spices are added; the okra supplies the hotness.

PREPARATION TIME: 15 minutes

COOKING TIME: 20-30 minutes

SERVES: 4 people

450-750g (1-1½lb) okra
Oil for deep frying
15ml (1 tblsp) oil
1 large onion, peeled and chopped
Salt and freshly ground black pepper to taste

Top and tail the okra; chop them into 5mm (¼ inch) even-sized pieces. Heat the oil for deep frying; add the chopped okra, a little at a time, and deep fry until brown and crisp. Drain on absorbent paper and keep warm in a dish. Heat the 15ml (1 tblsp) oil and fry the onion until tender about 4-5 minutes. Remove the onion and mix with the fried okra. Sprinkle with salt and pepper to taste. Serve with chapati, or as a side dish.

Aubergine Bake

PREPARATION TIME: 30 minutes

COOKING TIME: 30-40 minutes

SERVES: 6 people

3 large Dutch aubergines
10ml (2 tsp) salt
Malt vinegar
30ml (2 tblsp) oil
2 large onions, peeled and sliced
2 green chillies, chopped
425g (15oz) can peeled tomatoes, chopped
2.5ml (½ tsp) chilli powder
5ml (1 tsp) crushed garlic
2.5ml (½ tsp) ground turmeric
Oil for deep frying
60ml (4 tblsp) natural yogurt
5ml (1 tsp) freshly ground black pepper
4 tomatoes, sliced
225g (½lb) Cheddar cheese, grated

Cut the aubergines into 5mm (¼ inch) thick slices. Lay in a shallow dish. Sprinkle with 5ml (1 tsp) salt and add sufficient malt vinegar to cover. Allow to marinate for 20-30 minutes. Drain well. Heat 30ml (2 tblsp) oil in a frying pan and fry the onions until golden brown. Add the chillies, chopped tomatoes, remaining salt, chilli powder, garlic and turmeric. Mix well and simmer for 5-7 minutes. Remove from the heat. Cool and blend to a smooth sauce in the liquidiser. Keep the sauce on one side. Heat the oil for deep frying and deep fry the drained, marinated aubergine until brown on both sides (2-3 minutes each side). Drain well on kitchen paper. Grease a large deep baking tray. Arrange half the fried aubergine rounds closely together in the tray. Spoon over half the tomato sauce and beaten yogurt. Season with pepper. Add the remaining aubergine rounds and the rest of the tomato sauce and yogurt. Cover with slices of tomatoes and grated cheese. Bake at 180°C, 350°F, Gas Mark 4, for 10-15 minutes, or until the cheese melts and turns brown. Serve hot as a side dish, or as a main course with brown bread or pitta bread.

Stuffed Courgettes

This is a delightful dish from Southern Italy.

PREPARATION TIME: 30 minutes

COOKING TIME: 30-40 minutes

SERVES: 4 people

50g (2oz) fresh coarse breadcrumbs
60ml (4 tblsp) milk
8 medium sized courgettes, trimmed
1 onion, peeled and finely chopped
2 tomatoes, chopped
6-8 mushrooms, sliced
1 clove garlic, peeled and chopped
60ml (4 tblsp) olive oil
10ml (2 tsp) dried oregano
Salt and freshly ground black pepper to taste
1 egg, beaten
75g (3oz) Mozzarella cheese (or Cheddar), cut into thin slivers
75g (3oz) grated Parmesan cheese

Soak the breadcrumbs in the milk for 15-20 minutes. Cook the courgettes in boiling water for 5 minutes. Drain and cool. Slice them in half lengthways and scoop out the flesh, leaving a thick shell at least 5mm (¼ inch). Take care not to break or crack the courgettes.

This page: Aubergine Bake (top left), Okra Curry (centre right) and Okra Fry (right).

Overleaf: Courgette Bake (left), Stuffed Courgettes (centre) and Spicy Corn (right).

Keep the scooped flesh on one side. Squeeze out the excess milk from the breadcrumbs and put them into a bowl. Fry the scooped courgette flesh, chopped onion, tomatoes, mushrooms and chopped garlic in half the olive oil for 5 minutes. Mix with the breadcrumbs, oregano, salt and pepper to taste, the beaten egg and half the cheeses. Spoon the mixture evenly into all the courgette shells. Arrange the stuffed courgettes on a lightly greased baking tray. Sprinkle the remaining cheese over them and brush with the rest of the oil. Bake for 18-20 minutes at 200°C, 400°F, Gas Mark 6, or until the cheese has melted and turned golden brown. Serve at once.

Spicy Corn

This dish originates from East Africa, it makes a tasty hot snack or supper dish.

PREPARATION TIME: 15 minutes

COOKING TIME: 35-40 minutes

SERVES: 6 people

45ml (3 tblsp) oil
1 large onion, peeled and chopped
2 medium potatoes, peeled and cubed
8 fresh curry leaves (optional)
2.5ml (½ tsp) cumin seed
2.5ml (½ tsp) mustard seed
5ml (1 tsp) crushed fresh root ginger
5ml (1 tsp) crushed garlic
750g (1½lb) frozen sweetcorn kernels
5ml (1 tsp) salt
5ml (1 tsp) chilli powder
5ml (1 tsp) ground coriander
2.5ml (½ tsp) ground turmeric
425g (15oz) can peeled tomatoes, chopped
15ml (1 tblsp) tomato puree
1-2 green chillies, chopped
2 green peppers, seeded and cut into 2.5cm (1 inch) pieces
3 sprigs fresh green coriander, chopped
15ml (1 tblsp) thick tamarind pulp, or
30ml (2 tblsp) lemon juice

Heat the oil and fry the onion for 3 minutes; add the potatoes and fry for 5 minutes. Add the curry leaves, cumin and mustard seed and stir fry for 1-2 minutes. Add ginger and garlic and stir fry for 1-2 minutes. Add the sweetcorn, salt, chilli powder, ground coriander and turmeric. Mix well and cook for 2-3 minutes. Add the chopped

tomatoes, tomato puree, chopped chillies, green peppers and coriander leaves. Stir in the tamarind pulp and mix well adding a little water if the mixture seems too dry. Cover and cook over a low heat until the potatoes are tender about 10-15 minutes. The spicy corn should be thick but moist. Serve hot or cold.

Spiced Peas

PREPARATION TIME: 10 minutes

COOKING TIME: 15 minutes

SERVES: 6 people

30ml (2 tblsp) oil
1 large onion, peeled and chopped
2 green chillies, sliced in half lengthways
1kg (2lb) shelled peas (fresh or frozen)
Salt and freshly ground black pepper to taste
15ml (1 tblsp) lemon juice
Lemon wedges

Heat the oil in a wok or solid based frying pan and fry the onion until tender. Add the chillies and fry for 1 minute. Add the peas and salt and pepper to taste; stir fry for 5-10 minutes, or until well coloured and "dry". Put into a serving dish and sprinkle with lemon juice. Garnish with lemon wedges. Serve as a side dish, or as a snack.

Spinach with Paneer

Paneer is a home-made cheese; it is made by separating milk into curds and whey by means of a souring agent such as lemon juice. It is eaten extensively in northern parts of India and is a good source of protein.

PREPARATION TIME: 15 minutes, plus time for making paneer

COOKING TIME: 20-30 minutes

SERVES: 4 people

To make paneer: (This is an overnight process)
1.2 litres (2 pints) milk
30ml (2 tblsp) lemon juice

Bring the milk to the boil. Reduce the heat and sprinkle with the lemon juice. The milk will separate into pale watery whey and thick white paneer (or curds). Remove from the heat and allow the paneer to coagulate (if the milk has not

separated properly, add a few more drops of lemon juice. The whey should be a clear, pale, yellow liquid. Pour the paneer and liquid through a muslin-lined sieve. Discard the liquid whey and tie the muslin over the paneer. Flatten the paneer to 1cm (½ inch) thick; place it on a tray and rest it in a tilted position. Place more muslin over the top and weight it down. The pressure will drag out the remaining moisture and the tilted position will channel the liquid away from the paneer. Leave to drain overnight. Next day, cut the firm paneer into 2.5cm (1 inch) cubes.

75g (3oz) butter
1 medium onion, peeled and finely chopped
2.5cm (1 inch) piece cinnamon stick
1 bayleaf
450g (1lb) frozen spinach puree, or fresh leaf spinach, cooked and pureed
5ml (1 tsp) chilli powder
2.5ml (½ tsp) salt
120g (4½oz) natural yogurt
3 sprigs fresh green coriander leaves, chopped
5ml (1 tsp) garam masala powder
Oil for deep frying

Heat the butter in a pan and fry the onion until golden brown. Add the cinnamon and bayleaf and fry for 1 minute. Add the spinach and stir to mix. Sprinkle with the chilli powder and salt and stir in the yogurt, coriander leaves and garam masala. Cover and cook for 2-3 minutes. Simmer gently. Meanwhile, deep-fry the drained paneer cubes until golden. Add the paneer cubes to the spinach and simmer together for 4-5 minutes. Serve hot with chapati or pulao rice.

New Potato Fry

This Oriental dish is very versatile; it can be served as a side dish, as a snack, or as a main curry.

PREPARATION TIME: 20 minutes

COOKING TIME: 10-12 minutes

SERVES: 3-4 people

45ml (3 tblsp) oil
5ml (1 tsp) mustard seed
450g (1lb) small, even sized new potatoes, boiled in their skins and peeled

5ml (1 tsp) red chilli powder
7.5ml (1½ tsp) ground coriander
1.25ml (¼ tsp) ground turmeric
2.5ml (½ tsp) salt
3 sprigs fresh green coriander leaves, chopped (optional)
Lemon juice to taste

Heat the oil in a wok or solid based frying pan and add the mustard seed and the whole, peeled potatoes. Stir fry over a low heat until they are lightly browned. Sprinkle with the spices, salt and chopped coriander leaves. Stir fry over a low heat for 5-6 minutes until golden brown. Remove from heat. Put into a dish and sprinkle with the lemon juice. Serve hot or cold.

Courgette Bake

Serve this dish as a main course with fried rice, or as a side dish.

PREPARATION TIME: 20-30 minutes

COOKING TIME: 35 minutes

SERVES: 4-6 people

1kg (2lbs) courgettes, trimmed and coarsely grated
5ml (1 tsp) salt
30ml (2 tblsp) melted unsalted butter (or oil)
3-4 eggs, well beaten
175-200g (6-7oz) grated mild cheese (Edam, Samso, etc)
1 medium onion, peeled and finely chopped
2 cloves garlic, peeled and finely chopped
30ml (2 tblsp) chopped parsley
5ml (1 tsp) dried basil
2.5ml (½ tsp) freshly ground black pepper
30-40g (1-1½oz) grated Parmesan cheese

Put the grated courgettes into a colander and sprinkle with salt. Leave to drain for 10 minutes. Squeeze the moisture out of the

Facing page: Spiced Peas (top), Spinach with Paneer (centre right) and New Potato Fry (bottom).

courgettes until quite dry. Lightly grease a baking dish (size approx. 25cm x 18cm (10 inches x 7 inches). Heat the butter in a non-stick frying pan and fry the courgettes for 3-4 minutes until tender. Mix the beaten eggs, grated cheese, chopped onion, garlic, parsley, basil and pepper. Place the sauteed courgettes in the baking dish and pour egg mixture over the top. Sprinkle with the Parmesan cheese and bake at 180°C, 350°F, Gas mark 4, for 25-30 minutes until set. Serve cut into squares or diamond shapes. Can be eaten hot or cold.

Vegetable Stir Fry with Tofu

This is a Chinese stir fry dish with Tofu which makes a filling main course.

PREPARATION TIME: 30 minutes

COOKING TIME: 10 minutes

SERVES: 4 people

10ml (2 tsp) soya sauce
2.5cm (1 inch) fresh root ginger, peeled and thinly sliced
3 cloves garlic, peeled and crushed
225g (8oz) Tofu, cut into 1cm (½ inch) pieces
10ml (2 tsp) cornflour
200ml (⅓ pint) water
45ml (3 tblsp) oil
3 stems celery, sliced thinly
2 carrots, peeled and cut into thin diagonal slices
2-3 courgettes, trimmed, and cut into thin diagonal slices
1 green pepper, quartered, seeded and sliced thinly
8 mushrooms, thinly sliced
1-2 tomatoes, cut into wedges
50g (2oz) mange tout, or thinly sliced green beans

Mix the soya sauce with the Worcestershire sauce, ginger and garlic. Add the Tofu cubes and marinate for 8 minutes. Pick out the Tofu and keep on a plate. Stir the cornflour into the soya sauce mixture and blend in the water. Heat the oil in a wok over a medium heat. Add the celery and carrots and stir fry for 2 minutes. Add the courgettes and green pepper and stir fry for 2 minutes. Add the tomatoes and mange tout or green beans. Stir fry for 2 minutes. Add the mushrooms and stir fry for 1 minute. Stir in the

water and soya sauce mixture. Cook until thickened, stirring for 1-2 minutes. Add the Tofu. Heat through and serve immediately.

Cheese Bourag

PREPARATION TIME: 30-40 minutes

COOKING TIME: 20-25 minutes

SERVES: 4 people

225g (8oz) plain flour
Salt
7.5ml (3 tsp) baking powder
40g (1½oz) unsalted butter
120-150ml (4-5 fl oz) milk
225g (8oz) strong Cheddar cheese, grated
45ml (3 tblsp) chopped parsley
Oil for deep frying

Sieve the flour, 1.25ml (¼ tsp) salt and baking powder into a bowl; rub in the butter. Add the milk, a little at a time, and mix to a dough with a palette knife. Cover the dough and leave in a cool place to relax. Mix the grated cheese with the chopped parsley and a little salt to taste. Roll the dough out very thinly on a floured board and cut into 5cm (2 inch) squares. Brush the edges of half the squares with a dampened pastry brush. Place a little filling in the centre of each one and cover with the remaining squares. Seal the edges well by pinching with the fingers or notching with the prongs of a fork. Heat the oil for deep frying. Fry the bourags a few at a time in hot oil until golden and crisp. Drain on kitchen paper and serve hot with sweet and sour sauce.

Avial

This is a mixed vegetable dish made with coconut.

PREPARATION TIME: 30 minutes

COOKING TIME: 20 minutes

SERVES: 4 people

2 medium sized potatoes, peeled and cut into 2.5cm (1 inch) cubes
175g (6oz) lobia beans, trimmed and cut into 5cm (2 inch) pieces
50g (2oz) green beans, trimmed and sliced
4 drumstick or yard long beans, strung and cut into 2.5cm (1 inch) pieces
175g (6oz) squash, peeled and cut into 2.5cm (1 inch) cubes

1 green unripe banana, peeled and cut into 2.5cm (1 inch) pieces
1 aubergine, trimmed and cut into 2.5cm (1 inch) chunks
100g (4oz) shelled peas
½ fresh coconut, shelled, skin removed and thinly sliced
7.5ml (1½ tsp) cumin seeds
2 green chillies, chopped
120ml (4 fl oz) water
150ml (5oz) natural yogurt
45ml (3 tblsp) coconut oil for cooking

Steam all the vegetables for 10-15 minutes until almost tender, but still slightly crisp. Grind the spices with the water in a liquidiser until smooth. Mix the spice liquid with the coconut. Heat the coconut oil in a saucepan and add the vegetables, spice mixture and yogurt. Bring to the boil and simmer with the lid on for 5 minutes. Serve with rice.

Garlic Hash Brown

PREPARATION TIME: 20 minutes

COOKING TIME: 30 minutes

SERVES: 4 people

60ml (4 tblsp) oil
4 cloves of garlic, peeled and quartered lengthways
3 whole red chillies
Salt
450-750g (1-1½lb) potatoes, peeled and coarsely grated

Heat the oil in a wok or a large non-stick frying pan. Fry the garlic until lightly browned. Add the red chillies and fry for 30 seconds. Sprinkle with salt to taste and add the grated potato. Stir fry for 5 minutes. Cover and cook for a further 8-10 minutes. The potatoes should be crisp and golden brown. Cook until the potatoes are tender. Serve as a side dish or for breakfast.

Vegetable Stir Fry with Tofu (top), Avial (centre left) and Cheese Bourag (bottom right).

Spiced Chick Peas

This dryish curry is a "must" on any Punjabi menu. It is usually served with milk bread or pitta bread and an onion salad.

PREPARATION TIME: overnight overnight for soaking, plus 15 minutes

COOKING TIME: 40-50 minutes

SERVES: 4-6 people

450g (1lb) chick peas
5ml (1 tsp) baking powder
4 cloves
5ml (1 tsp) cumin seed
4 large black cardamoms, ground
4 small cardamoms, ground
1 large onion, peeled and chopped
45ml (3 tblsp) oil
2 bayleaves
2.5cm (1 inch) piece cinnamon stick
2 green chillies, sliced in half lengthways
2.5cm (1 inch) fresh root ginger, peeled and finely chopped
4 cloves garlic, peeled and crushed
7.5ml (1½ tsp) ground coriander
250-300ml (8-10 fl oz) canned tomatoes, chopped
2.5ml (½ tp) freshly ground black pepper
2.5ml (½ tsp) salt
5-6 sprigs fresh green coriander leaves, chopped

Wash the chick peas and soak them overnight in 1.2 litres (2 pints) water and the baking powder. The following day, cook the chick peas in their soaking liquid in a pressure cooker for 10-15 minutes. If a lot of liquid has been absorbed during soaking, add a little more. Dry roast the cloves and cumin seed in a frying pan. Grind the cloves, cumin, large and small cardamons into a fine powder. Fry the onion in the oil for 2-3 minutes. Add the bayleaves, cinnamon, chillies, ginger and garlic. Fry for 1 minute, add the ground coriander and tomatoes. Fry for 2-3 minutes. Strain the chick peas, retaining any liquid. Add the chick peas to the tomato mixture and add black pepper, salt and the dry roasted spices. Mix well and add 250ml (8 fl oz) of the strained chick pea liquid. Sprinkle with chopped coriander; cover and cook for 8-10 minutes. Add a little extra liquid if necessary. Serve with bread or rice.

Vegetable Pancakes (far left) and Spiced Chick Peas (left).

Vegetable Pancakes

A combination of shredded vegetables makes a delicious pancake, when added to the batter before cooking.

PREPARATION TIME: 15 minutes

COOKING TIME: 15 minutes

SERVES: 4-6 people

100g (4oz) butter
225g (8oz) shredded or coarsely grated carrots
225g (8oz) shredded or coarsely grated courgettes
450g (1lb) shredded or coarsely grated potatoes
1 medium onion, thinly sliced
3 eggs, well beaten
200ml (⅓ pint) soured cream
60ml (4 tblsp) cornflour
2.5ml (½ tsp) salt
2.5ml (½ tsp) freshly ground black pepper
Oil for frying
Wedges of lemon

Melt the butter in a frying pan; add the carrots, courgettes, potatoes and onion. Saute for 3-4 minutes, stirring continuously. Beat the eggs together with the soured cream, cornflour and salt and pepper. Mix well. Stir in the semi-cooked vegetables. Mix together gently. Heat a large non-stick frying pan and brush with 10ml (2 tsp) oil; add 15ml (1 tblsp) batter. Cook until light brown; turn the small pancake over and cook until the other side is also brown. Make 3 or 4 at a time. The size of the pancakes can be increased by using more batter for each pancake. Serve with salads or with tomato sauce as a light meal or snack.

Green Beans with Coconut

PREPARATION TIME: 10 minutes

COOKING TIME: 20 minutes

SERVES: 3-4 people

30ml (2 tblsp) oil
2 cloves garlic, peeled and crushed
2 green or red dried chillies
450g (1lb) green beans, sliced
1.25ml (¼ tsp) salt
30ml (2 tblsp) desiccated coconut, or grated fresh coconut

Heat the oil in a wok or frying pan. Add the garlic and fry until golden brown. Add the chillies and stir fry for 30 seconds. Add the green beans and sprinkle with salt. Stir fry for 8-10 minutes until the beans are tender but still crisp. Sprinkle with the coconut and stir fry for a further 2-3 minutes. Serve as a side dish.

Mixed Vegetable Raita

Raitas are yogurt-based Indian dishes served as accompaniments to curries etc. Natural yogurt is usually mixed with fruits, vegetables, and herbs such as coriander or mint.

PREPARATION TIME: 10 minutes

SERVES: 4-6 people

300ml (½ pint) natural yogurt
½ cucumber, chopped
1 small onion, peeled and chopped
2 tomatoes, chopped
2 stems celery, chopped
1 small apple, cored and chopped
2 boiled potatoes, peeled and chopped
1.25ml (¼ tsp) salt
1.25ml (¼ tsp) freshly ground black pepper
1 sprig fresh green coriander, chopped

Beat the yogurt in a bowl. Add all the remaining ingredients, seasoning well with salt and pepper. Chill before serving.

Cannelloni with Spinach and Ricotta

PREPARATION TIME: 20 minutes

COOKING TIME: 1 hour 20 minutes

SERVES: 4 people

30ml (2 tblsp) olive oil or melted butter
1 large onion, peeled and finely chopped
2 large cloves garlic, peeled and crushed
425g (15oz) can peeled tomatoes, chopped
15ml (1 tblsp) tomato puree
Salt and freshly ground black pepper to taste
7.5ml (1½ tsp) dried basil
2.5ml (½ tsp) dried oregano
350g (12oz) cannelloni tubes
60ml (4 tblsp) thick spinach puree
225g (8oz) Ricotta cheese
30ml (2 tblsp) grated Parmesan cheese

To make the sauce: heat the oil or butter and fry the onion and garlic for 2-3 minutes. Add the tomatoes and tomato puree and mix well. Simmer for 2 minutes. Add the salt and pepper, basil and oregano. Cover and simmer for 10-15 minutes until thick.

Bring a large pan of salted water to the boil; cook the cannelloni tubes for 10 minutes until just tender. Do not overboil. Lift out the cannelloni tubes and put them into a bowl of cold water to cool quickly. Drain well. Mix together the spinach, ricotta and salt and pepper to taste. Fill the cannelloni tubes with the spinach mixture and arrange them in a greased shallow ovenproof dish. Pour the tomato sauce over the cannelloni; sprinkle with the Parmesan cheese. Bake for 20-30 minutes at 180°C, 350°F, Gas Mark 4 or until the top is browned and bubbling. Serve at once.

Ginger Cauliflower

This is a very simple and extremely subtle vegetable dish spiced with ginger.

PREPARATION TIME: 15 minutes

COOKING TIME: 15 minutes

SERVES: 4 people

45ml (3 tblsp) oil
1 medium onion, peeled and chopped
2.5cm (1 inch) fresh root ginger, peeled and sliced
1-2 green chillies, cut in half lengthways
1 medium cauliflower, cut into 2.5cm (1 inch) florets, along with tender leaves and stalk
Salt to taste
2-3 sprigs fresh green coriander leaves, chopped
Juice of 1 lemon

Heat the oil in a wok or solid based saucepan; fry the onion, ginger and chillies for 2-3 minutes. Add the cauliflower and salt to taste. Stir to

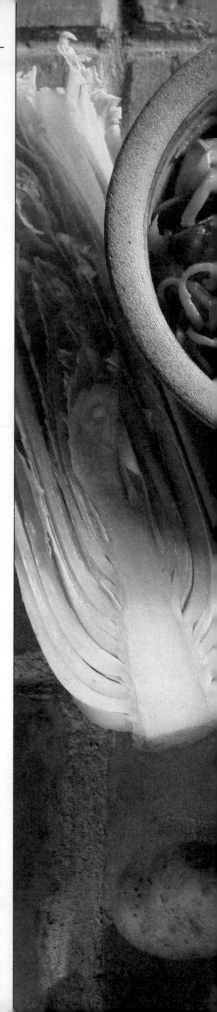

Noodles with Vegetables (top left), Green Beans with Coconut (centre right) and Garlic Hash Brown (bottom).

mix well. Cover and cook over a low heat for 5-6 minutes. Add the coriander leaves and cook for a further 2-3 minutes, or until the florets of cauliflower are tender. Sprinkle with lemon juice, mix well and serve immediately. Serve with pitta bread.

Mung Fritters

These tiny marble-sized fritters are made with mung pulse. They can be eaten as a cocktail snack or made into a curry with a well-flavoured sauce.

PREPARATION TIME: 1 hour 30 minutes

COOKING TIME: 30 minutes

SERVES: 4 people

225g (8oz) split mung pulse
1 small onion, peeled and chopped
5ml (1 tsp) chilli powder
7.5ml (1½ tsp) garam masala powder
2.5ml (½ tsp) cumin seed
4-5 sprigs fresh green coriander leaves, chopped
2.5ml (½ tsp) salt
Oil for deep frying

Wash and soak the mung pulse for 1 hour in sufficient cold water to cover. Drain and then grind into a thick coarse paste, adding 120-250ml (4-8 fl oz) water as you go. It should be the consistency of peanut butter. Mix the mung paste with the onion, chilli powder, garam masala, cumin seed, coriander leaves and salt. Mix well and adjust seasoning if necessary. Heat the oil for deep frying. Using a teaspoon, shape the paste into small "marbles" and fry in the hot oil until golden brown. Drain on kitchen paper and serve piping hot with chutney, a chilli sauce or a dip. To turn into a curry, add the Mung Fritters to the following curry sauce.

Sauce
10ml (2 tsp) oil
1 small onion, finely chopped
2.5ml (½ tsp) chilli powder
5ml (1 tsp) ground coriander
5ml (1 tsp) ground cumin
4-6 canned tomatoes, chopped
Salt to taste
3-4 sprigs fresh green coriander leaves, chopped

Heat the oil in a saucepan and fry the onion for 3 minutes. Stir in all the above ingredients; cover and

simmer for 5-8 minutes. Add a little water to make a thickish sauce. Add ready-fried Mung Fritters and simmer for 3-5 minutes.

Noodles with Vegetables

This exotic noodle dish can be served hot or cold, as a main course, as a side dish or as a snack.

PREPARATION TIME: 20 minutes

COOKING TIME: 30 minutes

SERVES: 4 people

Salt to taste
450g (1lb) egg noodles, or broken spaghetti
45ml (3 tblsp) oil
2.5cm (1 inch) fresh root ginger, peeled and thinly sliced
1 large or 2 medium onions, peeled and sliced
75g (3oz) green beans, sliced
75g (3oz) carrots, peeled and cut into matchstick strips
100g (4oz) white cabbage, or Chinese leaves, shredded
50g (2oz) shelled peas
75g (3oz) sprouting mung beans
1 green pepper, seeded and cut into 2.5cm (1 inch) pieces
1-2 stems celery, chopped
1-2 green chillies, split lengthways
2.5ml (½ tsp) monosodium glutamate (optional)
30ml (2 tblsp) soya sauce
15ml (1 tblsp) lemon juice
5-10ml (1-2 tsp) Chinese red pepper sauce
60ml (4 tblsp) chicken stock

Bring a large pan of water to the boil and add 5ml (1 tsp) salt. Add the noodles or spaghetti and boil gently for 5-6 minutes. Drain the noodles. Rinse the noodles in cold water and drain once again. Heat the oil in a wok or large frying pan. Fry the ginger for 1-2 minutes. Add the onions and fry for 2-3 minutes.

Add the beans and carrots and fry for 2 minutes. Add the remaining vegetables and the chillies and stir fry for 3-4 minutes. Add salt to taste and the noodles. Stir lightly with two forks. Dissolve the monosodium glutamate in the soya sauce and sprinkle over the noodle mixture; stir in the lemon juice, Chinese sauce and stock. Heat through for 2-3 minutes. Serve hot.

This page: Mung Fritters.

Facing page: Ginger Cauliflower (top left), Mixed Vegetable Raita (top right) and Cannelloni with Spinach and Ricotta (bottom).

Sauces, Dips and Chutney

Plum Chutney

Any variety of plum can be used; either singly or in a mixture of one or more varieties.

PREPARATION TIME: 10 minutes

COOKING TIME: 40 minutes

MAKES: about 3kg (6lbs)

2kg (4½lb) plums, pitted
2.5cm (1 inch) fresh root ginger, peeled and finely chopped
10ml (2 tsp) salt
1.5kg (3lb) brown sugar
5ml (1 tsp) cumin seed
5ml (1 tsp) coriander seed
4 dried red chillies
5ml (1 tsp) onion seed
30ml (2 tblsp) malt vinegar
50g (2oz) chopped blanched almonds
50g (2oz) chopped cashew nuts or hazelnuts
100g (4oz) raisins
100g (4oz) sultanas

Put the plums, ginger, salt and sugar into a saucepan, preferably a non-stick pan. Cover and cook gently until the plums are soft (about 15-20 minutes). Dry roast the cumin seed, coriander seed and red chillies in a frying pan for 1-2 minutes. Remove the red chillies and coarsely grind the cumin and coriander seeds. Add the roasted red chillies, ground spices and onion seed to the cooked plums. Add the malt vinegar, nuts, raisins and sultanas and simmer gently for 5-6 minutes. Allow to cool slightly. Pour into clean, warm glass jars and seal.

Guacamole
(AVOCADO DIP)

This is a popular Mexican dip, usually eaten with crisps, salty biscuits or sticks of raw vegetable, such as cucumber, celery etc.

PREPARATION TIME: 5 minutes

SERVES: 6-8 people

1 avocado, peeled, stoned and mashed
1 large clove garlic, peeled and crushed
5ml (1 tsp) salt

1.25ml (¼ tsp) freshly ground black pepper
1 large tomato, skinned and chopped
5ml (1 tsp) olive oil
15ml (1 tblsp) lemon juice
2-3 sprigs fresh green coriander leaves, finely chopped
1 small onion, peeled and grated

Blend the avocado pulp in the liquidiser with the salt, pepper, tomato, olive oil, lemon juice and coriander leaves. Put into a small bowl and mix with the onion. Serve with savoury biscuits, crisps or sticks of raw vegetables.

Tamarind Dip

PREPARATION TIME: 20 minutes

MAKES: about 400ml (⅔ pint)

75g (3oz) tamarind pods
250ml (8 fl oz) boiling water
2.5ml (½ tsp) salt
75-90g (3-3½oz) brown sugar
1 green chilli, chopped
1.25ml (¼ tsp) chilli powder

Soak the tamarind pods in boiling water for 5-6 minutes, or until soft. Rub the pods in the water to separate the dried pulp around the seeds. Squeeze out the seeds and skins of the pods. (Do not discard as a second extract can be obtained for future use). Add the salt and sugar to the tamarind pulp. Mix in the chilli and chilli powder and leave to stand for 5 minutes before using. Salt and sugar can be adjusted according to personal taste.

Savoury Coconut Chutney

PREPARATION TIME: 15 minutes

MAKES: about 450ml (¾ pint)

1-2 fresh coconuts, shell removed, outer skin peeled and cut into pieces
1cm (½ inch) fresh root ginger, peeled and chopped
2 green chillies, chopped
5ml (1 tsp) cumin seed

1-2 bunches fresh green coriander leaves, chopped
45ml (3 tblsp) thick tamarind pulp or
60ml (4 tblsp) lemon juice
5ml (1 tsp) sugar
2.5ml (½ tsp) salt

Put all the ingredients into the liquidiser and blend until smooth and creamy. If the mixture is too thick, add a little water.

Mixed Fruit Chutney

PREPARATION TIME: 30 minutes

COOKING TIME: 40 minutes

MAKES: about 2¼kg (5¼lb)

3 firm pears, cored and sliced
4 apples, cored and chopped
4 peaches, skinned, stoned and sliced or
425g (15oz) can peach slices, drained
450g (1lb) plums, halved and stoned
6 rings canned pineapple, cut into cubes
100g (4oz) dates, stoned and chopped
225g (8oz) dried prunes, soaked overnight
100g (4oz) dried apricots, soaked overnight
1kg (2¼lb) brown sugar
10ml (2 tsp) salt
2.5cm (1 inch) fresh root ginger, peeled and thinly sliced
100g (4oz) chopped blanched almonds
100g (4oz) cashew nuts, chopped
60ml (4 tblsp) malt vinegar
8 cloves, coarsely ground
5ml (1 tsp) chilli powder
5cm (2 inch) piece cinnamon stick
2 bananas, peeled and sliced

Put all the fruit into a saucepan (apart from the bananas) with the sugar, salt and ginger. Cover and cook for 15-20 minutes. Add the nuts, vinegar, cloves, chilli powder and cinnamon stick. Stir well and cook for 6-8 minutes. Simmer gently, stirring occasionally, until

most of the liquid has evaporated. The chutney should be thick and sticky. Add the sliced bananas and stir over the heat for 1 minute. Cool slightly. Pour into clean, warm glass jars and seal.

Green Tomato Relish

PREPARATION TIME: 4 hours

COOKING TIME: about 20 minutes

MAKES: about 1½kg (3lb)

1kg (2lb) green tomatoes, seeded and chopped
75g (6oz) shredded white cabbage
2 red peppers, seeded and chopped
1 onion, peeled and chopped
15ml (1 tblsp) salt
225g (8oz) brown sugar
300ml (½ pint) distilled white vinegar
10ml (2 tsp) mustard seed
10ml (2 tsp) celery seed
15ml (1 tblsp) prepared horseradish sauce

Mix the tomatoes, cabbage, peppers and onion together. Sprinkle with the salt and mix well. Leave to stand for 2-3 hours. Drain well and then rinse under cold running water. Drain and gently squeeze out the excess moisture. Mix the sugar, vinegar, mustard seed, celery seed and horseradish

Facing page: Plum Chutney (top right), Mixed Fruit Chutney (centre) and Green Tomato Relish (bottom).

Tamarind Dip (far left),
Savoury Coconut Chutney
(centre) and Guacamole
(Avocado Dip) (above).

Blend the parsley, garlic and vinegar in the liquidiser. Pour the parsley sauce into a small bowl and mix with the capers, olive oil, spring onions and salt and pepper. Mix well. Cover and chill for 10-15 minutes. The sauce can be thinned to the desired consistency with a little olive oil.

Chilli Sauce

This classic piquant sauce is perfect for those who love hot, spicy food.

PREPARATION TIME: 20 minutes	
COOKING TIME: 2 hours	
	30 minutes
MAKES: about 600ml (1 pint)	

8 large ripe tomatoes, skinned and
    chopped
2-3 small green peppers, seeded and
    chopped
2 medium onions, peeled and finely
    chopped
4 stems celery, chopped
10-15ml (2-3 tsp) salt
250g (9oz) granulated sugar
350ml (12 fl oz) cider vinegar
2-3 bay leaves
5ml (1 tsp) coriander seeds
5ml (1 tsp) freshly ground black
    pepper
1.25ml (¼ tsp) ground cloves
2.5ml (½ tsp) ground cinnamon
5ml (1 tsp) ground ginger
5ml (1 tsp) mustard seed

Mix all the ingredients together in a pan and bring to the boil. Cover and simmer for about 2 hours over a low heat, until thick. Stir once to mix and simmer again for 10 minutes. Remove from the heat and cool slightly. Pour into clean, warm glass jars and seal.

sauce together in a large solid based pan. Bring to the boil over a medium heat. Add the vegetables, cover and simmer gently for another 16-18 minutes until the relish is sticky. Remove from the heat and cool slightly. Pour into clean, warm glass jars and seal. Will keep for up to 2 months.

Mexican Salsa

This is a beautiful fresh sauce which goes well with curries and, of course, burritos and tacos.

PREPARATION TIME: 10 minutes	
MAKES: about 150ml (¼ pint)	

5 tomatoes, skinned and chopped
1 small onion, chopped
1-2 pickled or canned Mexican
    chillies, chopped
2 cloves garlic, peeled and crushed
10ml (2 tsp) malt vinegar
2.5ml (½ tsp) salt
2.5ml (½ tsp) sugar
2-3 sprigs fresh green coriander,
    chopped
5ml (1 tsp) bottled chilli sauce

Mix all the ingredients together in a bowl. Chill for 2 to 3 hours before serving.

Salsa Verde

A perfect Italian sauce to serve with any pasta, or with veal.

PREPARATION TIME: 15 minutes	
MAKES: about 200ml (⅓ pint)	

75ml (5 tblsp) chopped fresh parsley
30ml (2 tblsp) white wine vinegar
3 cloves garlic, peeled and sliced
30ml (2 tblsp) capers, finely chopped
30ml (2 tblsp) olive oil
2-3 spring onions, chopped
Salt and freshly ground black pepper
    to taste

This page: Chilli Sauce (top left), Salsa Verdi (centre) and Mexican Salsa (bottom).

Facing page: Rice Pudding (top), Potato Pudding (centre) and Cabbage Pudding (bottom).

Sweets

Carrotella

PREPARATION TIME: 15 minutes

COOKING TIME: 35-40 minutes

SERVES: 4-6 people

1.2 litre (2 pints) milk
450g (1lb) carrots, peeled and
    shredded
200ml (⅓ pint) canned evaporated
    milk
100g (4oz) granulated sugar
50g (2oz) raisins
Seeds of 8 small cardamoms, crushed
2 drops rose-water or vanilla essence
50g (2oz) chopped blanched almonds
50g (2oz) pistachio nuts, chopped

Put the milk into a pan and simmer
over a low heat until reduced to
900ml (1½ pints). Add the carrots;
cover and cook over a medium
heat for 15 minutes. Add the
evaporated milk, sugar and raisins.
Cover and simmer gently for
another 5 minutes. Remove from
the heat. Stir in the crushed
cardamom seeds and essence and
pour into a serving dish. Allow to
cool slightly. Sprinkle nuts on the
top and serve. On hot summer
days, the Carrotella is best chilled.

Carrot Cake

PREPARATION TIME: 30 minutes

COOKING TIME: 45-50 minutes

MAKES: 25cm (10 inch) loaf

175g (6oz) butter or margarine
175g (6oz) brown sugar
100g (4oz) granulated sugar
2 eggs, well beaten
225g (8oz) plain flour
7.5ml (1½ tsp) bicarbonate of soda
2.5ml (½ tsp) baking powder
1.25ml (¼ tsp) ground cinnamon
2.5ml (½ tsp) salt
225g (8oz) peeled carrots, shredded
75g (3oz) raisins
50g (2oz) chopped walnuts
1.25ml (¼ tsp) small cardamom
    seeds, crushed
Icing sugar for dredging

Cream the butter and sugars
together. Add the eggs, a little at a
time, beating well after each
addition. Sieve the flour,
bicarbonate of soda, baking
powder, cinnamon and salt
together. Fold the dry ingredients
into the egg mixture. Add the
carrots, raisins, nuts and crushed
cardamom. Mix well and pour the
mixture into a well buttered 25cm
(10 inch) loaf tin. Bake at 180°C,
350°F, Gas Mark 4, for 45-50
minutes, or until a fine metal
skewer comes out clean when
inserted into the centre of the cake.
Cool in the tin for 10-15 minutes,
before turning out. Dredge with
icing sugar before serving.

Rice Pudding

There are many ways of making a
rice pudding, but this is definitely
one of the best. It is suitable for
serving on any occasion, from
everyday meals to smart dinner
parties.

PREPARATION TIME: 10 minutes

COOKING TIME: 1 hour
                     30 minutes

SERVES: 6 people

50g (2oz) unsalted butter
1 bayleaf, crumbled
2.5cm (1 inch) piece cinnamon stick,
    crushed
175g (6oz) pudding rice, washed
    and drained
1.2 litre (2 pints) milk
400ml (⅔ pint) canned evaporated
    milk
175g (6oz) granulated sugar
50g (2oz) raisins
50g (2oz) chopped blanched almonds
50g (2oz) pistachio nuts, chopped or
    cut into slivers
Seeds of 8 small cardamoms, crushed

Melt the butter in a saucepan and
fry the bayleaf and cinnamon for 1
minute. Add the rice and stir well.
Add the milk and bring to the boil.
Reduce the heat and simmer for
40-50 minutes, stirring occasionally
to prevent the rice from sticking to
the pan. Add the sugar and
evaporated milk, and simmer for a
further 20-30 minutes, stirring
frequently. Thin layers of light
brown skin form on the base of the
pan, this is what gives the pudding
its rich reddish tinge and flavour.
Add the raisins and half the
chopped almonds. Mix well and
simmer for a further 5-10 minutes,
or until the pudding is really thick.
Mix in the crushed cardamom
seeds and pour into a serving dish.
Decorate with the remaining
chopped almonds and pistachio
nuts. Serve hot or cold.

Carrot Halva

A delightful sweet from the
mysterious East. Serve it hot or
cold, with or without cream.

PREPARATION TIME: 20 minutes

COOKING TIME: 50 minutes

SERVES: 8-10 people

2kg (4lb) large sweet carrots, peeled
    and shredded
900ml (1½ pints) canned
    evaporated milk
750g (1½lbs) granulated sugar
175g (6oz) unsalted butter
75g (3oz) raisins
Seeds of 10 small cardamoms,
    crushed
100g (4oz) chopped mixed nuts
    (blanched and chopped almonds,
    cashews, pistachios etc.)
Single cream

Put the carrots, evaporated milk
and sugar into a large solid based
pan and bring to the boil. Reduce
the heat and cook the carrots
gently for 30-40 minutes, or until
the milk has evaporated. Add the
butter and raisins and stir over a
gentle heat for 8-10 minutes, until
the Halva is dark and leaves the
sides of the pan clean. Add the
cardamom seeds and mix well. Pour
into a flat shallow dish about 2.5cm
(1 inch) deep. Flatten the Halva
evenly with a spatula. Sprinkle with
the chopped nuts. Serve hot or
cold, cut into squares, with single
cream.

Potato Pudding

This old-fashioned Oriental
pudding has a rich and lovely
flavour. It keeps for weeks and can
be frozen.

PREPARATION TIME: 15 minutes

COOKING TIME: 1 hour
                     15 minutes

SERVES: 6 people

1kg (2lb) potatoes, peeled and
    shredded
225g (8oz) unsalted butter
750ml (1¼ pints) canned
    evaporated milk
350g (12oz) granulated sugar
100g (4oz) ground almonds
1.25ml (¼ tsp) saffron
50g (2oz) chopped almonds and
    pistachios

Wash the potatoes thoroughly and
drain them well. Squeeze the
potatoes to remove all excess
moisture. Put the potatoes, butter
and evaporated milk into a large
solid based saucepan and cook
slowly until mushy. The potatoes
will disintegrate into a mashed
state as they cook. Add the sugar
and stir to dissolve. The mixture
will bubble and splatter like
bubbling mud from hot springs.
Wrap a damp tea towel around
your hand and stir the mixture for
20-30 minutes over a gentle heat.
Add the ground almonds and
saffron. Continue stirring over the
heat until the pudding becomes
thick, sticky and oily on the
surface. Pour the pudding into a
shallow dish and decorate with the
chopped nuts.

Cabbage Pudding

PREPARATION TIME: 10 minutes

COOKING TIME: 40 minutes

SERVES: 4-6 people

175g (6oz) finely shredded white
    cabbage
30ml (2 tblsp) pudding rice
1.2 litre (2 pints) milk

**Facing page: Carrot Cake
(top), Carrot Halva (centre)
and Carrotella (bottom).**

200ml (⅓ pint) canned evaporated
milk
2.5cm (1 inch) piece cinnamon stick
1 bayleaf
100-175g (4-6 oz) granulated sugar
50g (2oz) raisins
50g (2oz) chopped blanched almonds
50g (2oz) pistachio nuts, chopped
Seeds of 6 small cardamoms, crushed

Put the cabbage, rice, both milks,
cinnamon and bayleaf into a pan.
Bring to the boil and simmer gently
for 15-20 minutes, stirring
occasionally to prevent the mixture
from sticking to the pan. Add the
sugar and simmer gently until the
mixture is thick. Add the raisins
and nuts. Remove from the heat
when the rice is tender and the
milk has been reduced to approx.
600ml (1 pint). Pour into a serving
dish and sprinkle with the crushed
cardamom seeds. Mix well and
serve.

Frozen Lemon Yogurt Souffle

PREPARATION TIME: 20 minutes

SERVES: 4-6 people

900ml (1½ pints) natural yogurt
225g (8oz) caster sugar
Juice and finely grated rind of 2
lemons
5ml (1 tsp) vanilla essence
2 egg whites
1.25ml (¼ tsp) salt
1.25ml (¼ tsp) cream of tartar
120ml (4 fl oz) double cream,
whipped
Few thin lemon slices for decoration

Mix the yogurt, sugar, lemon juice,
lemon rind and vanilla essence
together. Whisk the egg whites, salt
and cream of tartar until stiff but
not dry. Fold the egg whites gently
into the yogurt mixture, and then
fold in the whipped cream. Pour
the mixture into a souffle dish and
freeze overnight. Garnish with
lemon slices before serving. Serve
either frozen or partially thawed.

Mango Fool

This delicious sweet can be made
with fresh or canned mangoes;
crushed cardamom seeds give it a
characteristic flavour.

PREPARATION TIME: 10 minutes

SERVES: 4-6 people

450g (1lb) canned mango slices or
the equivalent amount of fresh
mango, stoned and peeled
200ml (⅓ pint) canned evaporated
milk
Seeds of 6 cardamoms, crushed
Sugar to taste
Whipped cream

Put the mango, evaporated milk
and cardamoms into a liquidiser
and blend until smooth. Add a
little sugar if necessary. Pour into a
serving bowl and chill for 20
minutes before serving. Serve with
whipped cream.

Tropical Fruit Dessert

An exotic sweet dish to finish any
special meal. A delightful dessert
from nature's fruit garden.

PREPARATION TIME: 30 minutes

SERVES: 8-10 people

4 bananas, cut into 5mm (¼ inch)
thick slices
5 rings pineapple, cut into chunks
(fresh or canned)
2 semi-ripe pears, peeled, cored and
cut into chunks
2 medium red-skinned apples, cored
and cut into chunks
8 peach slices, chopped
225g (8oz) red cherries, pitted
45ml (3 tblsp) grated fresh coconut
1 honeydew melon, peeled and cut
into chunks
6-8 slices mango, cut into chunks
(fresh or canned)
2 kiwi fruit, peeled and cut into
chunks
20-25 strawberries, halved
Few seedless white and black grapes,
halved
15ml (1 tblsp) icing sugar
100g (4oz) cottage cheese
Few drops vanilla essence

Mix all the ingredients together in
a large bowl. Cover and chill for 1
hour.

Tropical Fruit Salad

This medley of fruits is very
colourful and it offers a variety of
tastes and textures.

PREPARATION TIME: 40 minutes

2 bananas, sliced
4 kiwi fruit, peeled and sliced
10 dates, stoned and sliced in half

2 guavas, halved and then sliced into
wedges
1 pawpaw, cut into thin crescent
shapes
450g (1lb) canned lychees, drained
225g (8oz) canned pineapple
chunks, drained (or pieces of fresh
pineapple)
2 fresh mangoes, peeled and sliced
Few seedless grapes, white and black,
halved
1 small melon, cut into chunks
¼ water-melon, cut into chunks
4 fresh figs, halved

Dressing
30ml (2 tblsp) lemon juice
Pinch salt
50g (2oz) chopped toasted walnut or
pine kernels

Prepare the fruits as suggested and
arrange in a large glass bowl, in
layers. Spoon over the lemon juice
and sprinkle with salt. Sprinkle
over the chopped nuts.

Semolina and Coconut Slices

PREPARATION TIME: 10 minutes

COOKING TIME: 30 minutes

SERVES: 6 people

175g (6oz) unsalted butter
175g (6oz) coarse semolina
225g (8oz) desiccated coconut
350g (12oz) granulated sugar
250ml (8 fl oz) canned evaporated
milk
250ml (8 fl oz) water
100g (4oz) chopped mixed nuts:
blanched almonds, cashews,
walnuts, hazelnuts and pistachios
75g (3oz) raisins
Seeds of 6 cardamoms, crushed

Melt the butter in a frying pan and
add the semolina. Dry roast the
semolina by stirring it until it turns
lightly golden. Spoon onto a plate.
Dry roast the coconut in the same
pan until lightly golden. Add the

**Tropical Fruit Dessert (top
right), Frozen Lemon Yogurt
Souffle (top left) and Tropical
Fruit Salad (bottom).**

semolina, sugar, milk and water to the coconut. Stir the mixture over the heat for 5-8 minutes. Add the chopped nuts, raisins and crushed cardamom seeds. Mix well and stir over a gentle heat for 5-6 minutes, until the mixture is thick and the oil begins to separate. Pour into a shallow dish, smooth with a spatula and allow to cool. Cut into diamond shapes or squares.

Mint Barley Sherbet

PREPARATION TIME: 10 minutes

COOKING TIME: 20 minutes

SERVES: 4-6 people

100g (4oz) whole barley
900ml (1½ pints) water
25g (1oz) mint leaves, minced
Pinch salt

75g (3oz) granulated sugar
Juice of 3 lemons
1-2 drops green food colouring
Grated rind of 1 lemon
Few mint leaves and lemon slices to decorate

Wash the barley in 2-3 changes of water. Soak the barley in the measured water for a few minutes; add the minced mint leaves and

This page: Yogurt, Almond and Saffron Sherbet (top centre), Mango Sherbet (left), Maori Shake (centre) and Tropical Blizzard (right).

Facing page: Mint Barley Sherbet (top left), Spiced Tea (top right) and Rich Coffee (bottom).